Endorsements

Meet Me Where I Am does just that, meeting you where you are. Cindy Sproles takes us back to scripture, encouraging us to study and reconnect with Christ more deeply. Her use of scripture and history helps us fall in love with Jesus, even more. This fantastic book will help you commit God's Word to your heart, just where you are.

—**Billie Jauss**, speaker, podcast host of *start small BELIEVE BIG*, and author of *Distraction Detox* and *Making Room*

I have realized over years of ministry that most people aren't used to reading, understanding, and applying the Bible to their own lives. In *Meet Me Where I Am, Lord*, Cindy Sproles helps us apply the Bible where we live day in and day out. Whether you are new to faith or just needing to see the Scriptures from a different angle, this book will help the Bible come alive in your own life.

—**Jason Warden**, senior minister, Farragut Christian Church, Knoxville, Tennessee

The roots of a tree have two primary jobs; they anchor the foundation and absorb life sustaining nutrients from the soil. In *Meet Me Where I Am, Lord*, Cindy K. Sproles provides followers of Jesus with a powerful tool for strengthening their spiritual roots. Her devotions, written for all audiences in any season of life, will assist you in reexamining and rejuvenating your relationship with God from the ground up. Using Scripture as her guide, Sproles takes the reader beneath the surface of religious superficiality to uncover who we are in Christ. This practical devotional work is a breath of fresh air for those who want to humbly reestablish a hunger for God and the spiritual nourishment His Word provides.

—**Chad Broaddus**, DMin, lead minister, First Church, Owasso, Oklahoma

90 DAYS TO KNOW HIM DEEPER

Meet me where I am, LORD

CINDY K. SPROLES

Birmingham, Alabama

Meet Me Where I Am, Lord

Iron Stream
An imprint of Iron Stream Media
100 Missionary Ridge
Birmingham, AL 35242
IronStreamMedia.com

Copyright © 2023 by Cindy K. Sproles

Library of Congress Control Number: 2022941946

Cover design by Hannah Linder Designs

ISBN: 978-1-56309-615-0 (paperback)
ISBN: 978-1-56309-616-7 (e-book)

1 2 3 4 5—27 26 25 24 23

Dedicated To

Ann Tatlock and Eddie Jones

Two individuals who have helped guide me through the years in
standing firm in a strong Christian worldview.

Contents

Foreword

I n the fall of 2019, I was playing golf with a friend when he asked about my most recent writing project. I had written a few nonfiction books about the church and pastoral ministry but was venturing into new territory—Christian historical fiction. "I feel like a fish out of water," I admitted after slicing another golf ball into the woods. "It's like nothing I've done before. Like I'm starting over from scratch as a writer. I'm a complete novice."

My friend thought for a moment, then said, "You need to meet Cindy Sproles."

Turns out I did need to meet Cindy Sproles. Once our mutual friend connected us, Cindy, an award-winning, best-selling novelist, patiently walked through my manuscript with me, sharpening my plot and teaching me about dialogue, suspense, and how to use descriptive language in a way that furthers a story rather than bogging it down. She was gracious, honest, and challenging. She made me a better writer.

Beyond her ability to write and to teach writing, I was most impressed with her heart for Jesus Christ. For Cindy K. Sproles, writing is a ministry. It's a way to glorify God by introducing Him to those who don't yet know Him and encouraging those who already walk with Him to grow more faithful in that walk. Her heart for and dependence on God shines through every page she writes.

I was thrilled when she told me she felt the Lord leading her to write a devotional book. In the midst of her steady stream of historical novels, she has developed a tool that aids believers in our daily rhythms of Bible reading, prayer, and reflection.

Long-term, substantive growth in faith depends heavily on these daily rhythms. As Jesus "often withdrew to lonely places and prayed" (Luke 5:16 NIV), His followers over the centuries have, likewise, incorporated daily disciplines into their faith that sustain them, nourish them, and grow them. *Meet Me Where I Am, Lord* provides a helpful companion to believers who may be developing or sustaining these Christlike rhythms.

The devotions in this book are insightful and accessible. Sproles provides bite-sized, understandable insights that, though read in just minutes, marinate in our hearts and minds throughout the day.

These devotions are biblical. Each entry grows from a passage of Scripture, and Sproles gives careful attention to each passage's context and grammar, interpreting Scripture with theological accuracy and consistency. As Paul bid Timothy, she "correctly handles the word of truth" (2 Timothy 2:15 NIV).

These devotions are helpful. After careful interpretation of Scripture, Sproles applies each passage to the questions, struggles, and issues that keep us awake at night. Page by page, she shows us how God's truth matters where we live; and, in fact, how it changes the ways we live. I've devoted over twenty-five years to church leadership and Christian higher education, and I've seen, time and again, the value and necessity of believers giving attention to their daily devotion.

We need not do it alone. Help is available. Writers and teachers like Cindy K. Sproles come alongside us on the journey of faith, equipping and encouraging us to thrive in our relationships with Jesus.

Therefore, I am pleased and honored to recommend *Meet Me Where I Am, Lord.*

Daniel Overdorf, DMin
professor of pastoral ministries
Johnson University
Knoxville, Tennessee
author of *A Death Well Lived*

Acknowledgments

While serving as an acquisitions editor, I have searched for years for a devotional that dug just a bit deeper than the surface—one that held firm to biblical teaching, without a "this is my opinion" included or the Word forced into a hobby or theme. As I sat talking to Suzanne Kuhn, an associate publisher with Iron Stream Media, and expressed how I'd just not found this type of devotional, she boldly said, "Why don't you write it?" I was speechless. Sometimes God has to shake us just a bit before we see the obvious. Perhaps the entire time I was searching, He was calling me to do the task. A special thank you to Suzanne for being that person who opened my eyes and then was willing to present this work to her publications board and approve it. Thank you, I am grateful for the gentle shake.

To Daniel Overdorf, professor of pastoral ministries and director of preaching programs at Johnson University in Knoxville, Tennessee, who agreed without hesitation to stand behind me and oversee each doctrinal detail of this work. It meant a great deal to me to have someone willing to serve in that headship position and assure that I have accurately and appropriately represented the Word.

To Bob Hostetler, who has stood by me as a prayer warrior, friend, and agent. I am grateful for his belief in me as a writer and a ministry leader. Thank you, Bob. You are a blessing to my family and me.

To Nancy Haga, who took the time to read through and honestly offer her thoughts on this book. Thank you just doesn't seem to be enough.

To my husband, sons, and their wives. Thank you for supporting my writing career. I work at this to remind you that even when we face difficulties within our lives—those bumps like cancer and hard knocks—you will see that our faith is the tie to overcoming the rocky spots and sailing on gentle breezes. God is faithful through every moment.

To the Thursday morning women's Bible study group at Colonial Heights Christian Church: Nylene Jones, Pat Wininger, Kim Elkins, Barbara Tilley, Ruth Goodwin, Jann Stamper, Phyllis Davidson, Barbara Holt, Allison Cathey, and Nancy Haga. You are my friends, mentors, "neighbors," and support system. Thank you so much. To say *I love you* is simply not enough.

And finally, to my Father in Heaven. Forgive me for being so deaf that I missed your whisper to do this project. May all the glory be Yours.

Much love,
Cindy

Introduction

I missed a good solid devotional. Not a niche devotional. Not a devotional that took a hobby or a life situation and forced Scripture to fit the situation. I'm talking meaty. Something that speaks to me regardless of the season of life I'm in, or even if my husband picks it up. Will it apply to him as well?

Perhaps I'm a little hard on the writing community. Having served as an acquisitions editor and managing editor for a publisher for over eight years, I suppose I was expecting more. Though there are some wonderful devotionals on the market, it seemed writers spent more time addressing the things wrong with their lives. Hardship with children, depression, disabilities, co-dependency. Those are good, but I needed more. I needed Him! I didn't need someone's idea of how to fix me. I wanted spiritual guidance.

With the Christian worldview vastly decreasing, where on earth were the devotions hiding that shoved me back into the Scripture? Back into study and absolutes? Back into relationship building with my Father. Not sweet. Not shallow. What I needed, longed for, and desired, was the Word. I was hungry to hear God teach, speak, and then apply it to my life.

Conference after conference, I stood in front of writers and offered this challenge. "Think of meaty. I want to put us back into the Word of God where we can meet up with the Father." After three years of asking, one young writer stepped up. We contracted her and published thirty devotions in the Word. After that . . . nothing. Plea after plea, and no other author took the challenge. I had to wonder why? Was delving into the Word too hard? Did the challenge, with a contract practically attached, not entice anyone? My thoughts were that writers were trying to fit God into a box, and God is un-fittable. Then it happened.

The challenge came back to me. "Why don't you write it?" Honestly, it hadn't crossed my mind. Had I been so busy searching that I missed the nudge God was offering? I realized I wasn't listening spiritually.

I took on the challenge, and as I began, I could see how God had placed specific people in my path who could help me remain biblically sound in the doctrine and accountable in the work. With no agenda other than laying out the Scripture placed on my heart, I took on the challenge of studying to show myself approved. If no one else met the need, I would heed the call.

This devotional needed to be meaty but not hard to absorb. It needed to be doctrinally sound and biblically available. It required teaching but not preaching. And challenges but not overzealous expectations. And so, I began to write with this prayer.

> *Lord, I am the pen. You are the Word. Use this to Your glory. Father, meet me where I am, for I am far from where I should be.*

I hope you will find a new perspective in your relationship with Christ as you walk through these devotions. I hope you will learn a bit more than simply scratching the surface. I pray that you won't look for fancy words or monumental revealing moments, but rather you will take hold of the Word of God, dig just a little deeper, and apply each day to your life. Grow in your understanding and your relationship with the *Great I Am*.

If you ask, *Meet Me Where I Am, Lord*, He will.

Week 1—Who You Are in Christ

Restoring a solid Christian worldview in our lives begins in the basement. The very basics—knowing who we are in Christ. Often it's not that we don't know these things. It's that the world has so skewed what we once knew in the depths of our souls. It means revisiting exactly what truth is.

In John 18:37–38, Pilate arrogantly flings the question, "'So you are a king?' Jesus answered, 'You say that I am a king. For this purpose I was born and for this purpose I have come into the world—to bear witness to the truth. Everyone who is of the truth listens to my voice.' *Pilate said to him, 'What is truth?'*" (emphasis on this page is mine).

How many times have we read the account of Jesus before Pilate and not truly absorbed the proclamation Jesus makes? "For this purpose I was born and for this purpose I have come into the world—to bear witness to the *truth*" (John 18:37). Our minds can begin to connect the dots with other scripture that supports this proclamation, "I am the way, and the *truth*, and the life" (John 14:6). "In the beginning was the Word, and the Word was with God, and the Word was God" (John 1:1). And the proof of who and what is *truth* goes on and on throughout the New Testament.

For us to reestablish a strong Christian worldview, we must find out who we are in Christ, and once we see that, we must believe it. Learning to discern the world's desires against the desires of God in us can be difficult. The world makes a compelling argument for its selfish ways. It works hard to discredit what we believe by the simple act of desensitizing us. We know this. The demise of our beliefs has not been a sudden thing but rather a slow picking away over time.

In week one, study these scriptures and meditate over them. Let them lead you to who you are in Christ. Let them help you begin to reestablish a hunger for the Word. Long for your relationship with Christ, for He longs for His relationship with you.

You will have to work at it because the forces of evil will fight against you. Take this with you this week as you study and pray.

Day 1

Therefore, preparing your minds for action, and being
sober-minded, set your hope fully on the grace that
will be brought to you at the revelation of Jesus Christ.
—1 Peter 1:13

Being moved to action can sometimes be challenging. Fear enters. What will others think if I take action on a particular event? Will I be judged, punished, or ridiculed when my decision to speak loudly comes? When we decide the time is right to move, we must be sure our motives are pure and righteous, not overtaken by sudden emotion or misled by the chants and cries of others. It's easy to be swept up in the passion and emotion of the crowd.

Still, it seems the majority of the time, when we are ready to take action, it is on a deeper and more personal level. Others often see our efforts to change our lives in ways we cannot imagine. Peter tells us our minds should be prepared, that our thoughts are clearheaded, and our motives and desires are right.

Peter understood this. It was he who was always quick to jump, somewhat overprotective, and at times quick-tempered. It must have genuinely shaken him from the inside out when Jesus called him the rock. Peter, the rock, suddenly remembered his place on earth. Commissioned. Determined. And maybe a little unsure. Peter began to prepare to pull his emotions into check and be that sober-minded, wise rock from which the earthly church would spring.

Taking action is not always in a large arena. Instead, it is on our knees at the foot of our bed, humbled before the God who has saved us. Taking action in our personal lives allows us to grasp hold of that grace freely given by Christ Jesus.

Day 2

Therefore encourage one another and build one another up,
just as you are doing.
—1 Thessalonians 5:11

We live in ruthless times. Every turn holds a trapdoor that, when stepped on, drops us into a place of despair. Men wave flags and shout they are abused and repressed, yet their concern is only for themselves—for in the same breath, they will tear their brother down. Should we stand and look head-on into the abyss, we might feel there is no hope, but the truth is that things are no different now than they were when Paul wrote to the Thessalonians.

Man is a selfish sort, always seeking his well-being first. Paul wanted the people to step above the ridicule of others' selfishness, greed, and lack of consideration. Being a positive light may be the only light someone sees for the day. Encouragement lifts the spirit of the downtrodden. It is a tool of reliance. When we learn to encourage, others look to us as support. They will lean on us, and then the opportunity to show how we rely on Christ gives us peace and hope.

Our vulnerability to lean on Him for all our needs, guidance, peace, and hope leads others to want what we have when they see our dependence and reliance on Christ. Encourage. Build others up for it strengthens your relational foundation as well as that of those who are onlookers.

Day 3

Put on then, as God's chosen ones, holy and beloved, compassionate
hearts, kindness, humility, meekness, and patience, bearing with one
another and, if one has a complaint against another, forgiving each
other; as the Lord has forgiven you, so you also must forgive.
—Colossians 3:12–13

From the beginning, man was self-centered. His faithfulness and
ability to trust were weak, even back to the garden. Humanity
sways easily, and the Father knows this weakness in us. Through the
centuries, God has remained faithful, forgiving, and sufficient for us. His
willingness to forgive our sin is an example of His immense love. So why
is it so hard for us to forgive others when the Father continues to offer us
grace and mercy?

Perhaps for humanity, forgiving others leads to a weaker version of
who we are. Maybe our inner sinful selves refuse to let go of the wrongs
others have done. Yet refusing forgiveness for others prevents us from
reaching a higher plane in our walk with God. It is often said the act
of forgiving others is not for those who receive, though it offers a sense
of renewal and an opportunity to start over. Instead, forgiveness is for
the forgiver. It is for us so that our souls release the anger, hurt, and
frustration that stands in our way of a stronger, healthier relationship with
the Father. How can we function in harmony with the Father when we
refuse to release the bonds that tie us to our sin and circumstance?

Christ proved the perfect example of forgiveness when He hung on
the cross and cried out to His Father and God, "Forgive them." Forgive
them—what powerful words to live by.

Whatever you do, work heartily, as for the Lord and not for men,
knowing that from the Lord you will receive the inheritance as your
reward. You are serving the Lord Christ.
—Colossians 3:23–24

Often, we become lost in our own provision. Making our own way. There are times it seems the harder we work, the more the accomplishment of the task is unreachable—futile. Our focus is on pleasing man rather than striving for the relational pleasure of God. The work we do becomes something we own rather than offering the effort fully to the glorification of God. Scripture is clear, "Whatever you do, work heartily, as for the Lord and not men."

When our efforts, be they personal, career oriented, or relational, are focused inwardly, the work becomes self-centered and self-gaining. But when our work, whatever the work may be, is done well and done for God and His glory, He rewards us spiritually. We receive a sense of fulfillment and contentment. There is great joy in the completion of a task handed over to God. This is when our efforts become a service to God, offering a multitude of ways He can work both in and through what we have done. Earthly rewards are a sweet pat on the back, but the rewards built in the kingdom satisfy the hunger for self-gratification. God supplies the perfect gifts for those who serve Him faithfully. Rejoice in your work even when it is difficult. Offer it in full to the service of God. Your efforts will not go unnoticed.

Day 5

The heavens declare the glory of God, and the sky above
proclaims his handiwork. Day to day pours out speech,
and night to night reveals knowledge.
—Psalm 19:1–2

Worship is a personal part of our visible relationship with the Father. His remarkable feats of creation are all around us, yet we worship the creation rather than the Creator. Our worship should feed into our souls and leave us with genuine love, thanksgiving, and hope. God is very aware of all He has made, including each individual He lovingly knit together. What He requires of us is our attention. Our gratitude. Our love. We do that through our worship of Him, or when we look into the heavens and see the vastness of His universe. There is the promise of hope in the stars that are light years away. Even in the sunrise, we see His promises of new life. In the song of a bird, we feel His nearness. It is easy to understand why the psalmist spoke that the heavens declare the glory of God. It cannot be denied. There is absolution within that one view that God is God, for we cannot look into His creation without recognizing who God is.

Look at every point of the Father's creation and worship He who created it. For in our worship, our relationship with Him tightens, the depth of how we know Him grows. Here we find peace, mercy, and grace. His handiwork shouts His glory, and we can bask in that glory, praise Him, and worship Him wholeheartedly. The Lord God is mighty.

Day 6

If you then, who are evil, know how to give good gifts to
your children, how much more will the heavenly Father
give the Holy Spirit to those who ask him!
—Luke 11:13

Difficult times seem to be the most common ones to ask the Father for the pleas of our hearts. It seems we only realize what is available to us through prayer when we are in distress. Of course, the Father adores His children. As a loving father, God never wants His children to be in need. The psalmist understood that when he penned Psalm 23:1 and declared, "The Lord is my shepherd; I shall not want." His love abounds, yet as His children, we rarely accept the gifts He has already given us—gifts filled with amazing prayer. What about the gift of the Holy Spirit? What of the power and intercession held within this gift?

Luke uses the example of sinful men and how they provide or give to their children, and he compares that, multiplied, by the heavenly Father who offers us the Holy Spirit. We only have to ask. Yet, how often do we ask to use this gift He freely has given? Imagine the depth of love found within the confines of the Holy Spirit. Imagine the flames that burned above the heads of the disciples as they received this gift. Then picture praying with the fire of the Holy Spirit and seeing the gates of heaven open in your soul.

Our God is mighty, and the love for His children is unconditional, undying, and faithful. If man would seek to give great things to their children, look how much more the God of the universe gives when we simply ask in His name. The gifts are free. Learning to access them means learning to submit. "Ask, and it will be given . . . seek, and you will find; knock, and it will be opened to you" (Matthew 7:7) and welcome a deeper, more significant relationship with Him.

Day 7

But our citizenship is in heaven, and from it we
await a Savior, the Lord Jesus Christ.
—Philippians 3:20

Paul felt strongly about getting this message across. As Christians, our "conversation," citizenship, country, and home, is heaven. Though earth is our physical home, everything about us should be as we would be in heaven. That's something to dwell over—everything we say or do should be said or done as if we were in heaven. Difficult? Most certainly. As humans, it is hard to look past what is temporal to what is eternal. We stand, knuckles whitened, grasping tightly to all that is earthly, struggling to loosen our grip so we might grasp instead where our Savior waits for us. Still, Paul states a strong case, reminding us of the gift that awaits us.

So how does this shape our current selves? It gives us cause to look deeper at our hearts and where or what we stand firm over. Are our feet planted solidly on the boundaries of heaven, or are we still willing to cling to the things that will only bring us temporary joy—even pain?

The joy of what is to come for the Christian should most certainly burn in our hearts. Remember the moment you went under the forgiving and cleansing waters of baptism? That joy, that freedom from the bonds of sin, that moment when you let go of what was earthly, and your citizenship turned heavenly. For some, it was only momentary, but for others long lasting. You as a child of God have citizenship in heaven. Focus on what is eternal, for that is the ultimate goal.

Week 2—What We Receive from Christ

To narrow down the multitude of things we receive from Christ is unfair. There are so many, and these verses are only the beginning. First we asked, "Who are we in Christ?" We continue by adding a few of the things we receive from Christ. There is so much, but we begin again in the basement with the basics.

Our understanding of who we are in Christ grows as we develop a deep and continued relationship with Him. By that same token, wrapping our heads around the gifts God presents us with daily is hard. Our first challenge is to believe these things are accessible to us and free. Then secondly, we must understand that they are given unconditionally. He gives us citizenship, protection, compassion, love, and discipline.

These things are easy to filter from our daily lives because of our do-it-myself attitude. We don't need help—until we do. We don't need to release our independence and bow in submission. Therefore, accepting God's loving-kindness can be difficult.

The scriptures in the coming week are only the beginning of what God offers us. But understanding truth means we begin to define and accept these gifts. The world tries to tell us we are unworthy of these gifts, and often we fall into the belief that this is true. After all, why would the God of the universe want to love such an imperfect person? This is a lie of the world. But wait, we might ask, "Who is the world?" The answer is simple. *We* are the world. Man in his weak state easily accepts the lies we tell ourselves. The Prince of Darkness knows how to veer us away, and he begins by telling us we are unworthy. When this lie penetrates your heart, remember you *are* worthy. God didn't send His son to die for a soul He felt was unworthy. You are worthy. Take in His gifts.

Day 8

Fear not, little flock, for it is your Father's good
pleasure to give you the kingdom.
—Luke 12:32

What an endearing title Jesus chose to use. "Little flock." His reference is clear. Man must be guided, led, watched over, and more so—that He is our overseer, guide, and shepherd. Jesus was concerned about the things that could mislead the people. Looking ahead for believers now, it is those who skew the truth of Christ with keenly hidden hypocrisy. It's our worry about what men think of us, over what God would think. Worse yet, a failure to acknowledge or proclaim God. These are all prominent issues that faced believers in Luke's time and equally now. Even as we worry, so did the people then. Their concerns for the basics of life like food and clothing needed the same type of trust required of us today. It's easy to say God will provide for His children, but the question becomes do we believe He will do as He promised?

It is frightening when we look at what the world can do to us physically and mentally. Our confidence may wane. How can we evade sin when it is so plainly pushed at us? Jesus gently reminded the people, "Don't fear, little flock." All the hard things that surround you are nothing in the hands of the Father who loves you and finds pleasure in giving you the kingdom. In other words, He gives His all to your care.

The picture Christ painted of the shepherd who sought after the one sheep which was lost is perfect comfort. God knows every hair on our head, every need, every hurt, and He freely cares for us with all He has. When the world presses down hard, "Fear not, little flock," for it is His pleasure to care for you.

Day 9

This Book of the Law shall not depart from your mouth, but you shall meditate on it day and night, so that you may be careful to do according to all that is written in it. For then you will make your way prosperous, and then you will have good success.
—Joshua 1:8

Joshua had big shoes to fill. As Moses's assistant, God moved Joshua into Moses's place of leadership after his death, but not without first offering Joshua encouragement. God reminded Joshua that His promise made to Moses would be honored—the promised land would belong to them, no enemy would withstand them, and He (God) would always be with him. God finished this charge with instructions to meditate on the Book of the Law day and night, so Joshua was careful to obey. Do that, and your way will be prosperous. Successful.

It is easy for us to apply these spiritual promises to ourselves, but remember, these promises were meant for the people of Israel. We cannot assume that because God promised this land to Israel, He will promise us land, a title, or even a spouse. We can take from this historical account the faithfulness of God and that His promises are real. Our experiences work toward our eternal inheritance, and even when we face hardships, the Enemy cannot withstand us when we have Christ. Furthermore, no believer has gotten up one morning to find God has forsaken them. God is faithful, true to His Word, and He is always available to us. Even as He has offered us promises through Christ Jesus, God still asks for our love and insists on obedience. Meditate on His words. The Word is timeless and always applicable. God has not changed. His promises are still perfect and true.

11

> He said to him the third time, "Simon, son of John,
> do you love me?" Peter was grieved because he said to him the third
> time, "Do you love me?" and he said to him, "Lord, you know
> everything; you know that I love you."
> Jesus said to him, "Feed my sheep."
> —John 21:17

Peter must have been brokenhearted when Jesus asked him not once but three times if he loved him. It might seem fair that Jesus repeatedly asked, especially since Peter had denied knowing Jesus three times. Some might say it was ironic Jesus would ask three times, but perhaps He wanted to be sure Peter's boastfulness had left.

How often must we be reminded if we love Jesus? Jesus knew Peter loved Him, but it bore significance for Peter. He needed to answer this question. It was imperative that Peter understood Jesus forgave him since Jesus would soon ascend to heaven. It is also crucial that Jesus asks Peter to care for His earthly flock. Peter, one who questioned much, needed to hear and see this forgiveness. The fact that Jesus's love and forgiveness extended far beyond Peter into us, in and of itself, is an amazing thing. Just as Jesus knew everything about Peter, likewise He knows us. When this question is posed to us, it forces us to reexamine our relationship with the Father. How much do we love Him, and how deep is our devotion to the God who never walks away from us—even when *we* walk away from Him.

Ponder this. Imagine Christ standing next to you, gently pressing His hand onto your shoulder. Place your name in this sentence and hear Him ask, "_____, do you love me?" Feel His conviction and reach to Him for the forgiveness every man needs, and then reply, "Yes, Lord, I love you." So then, feed His sheep.

As a father shows compassion to his children, so the Lord
shows compassion to those who fear him.
—Psalm 103:13

When we hear the words "those who fear the Lord," it's easy to assume this refers to those who cower, quake, and quiver with fear. Does this mean that God only shows compassion for those who shake at His presence?

The answer is an unequivocal no. It is sometimes difficult to fully comprehend the expanse of God's love, much less how He could love even the sinner. Still, the Father knows our weaknesses and understands those are the things that cause us to fall and flounder. Since we are all His children, His compassion reaches gently down to cover us from what may deter us from walking in the light. The mercy of God is grand, and though He knows those who come to Him are frail by heavenly terms, He loves us fully. His heart yearns to lift his children from the "miry bog" (Psalm 40:2).

As a father who sees his child fall and then reaches out to offer refuge, so does the Father of all do for His children. The psalmist fully described the mighty power of God's love as "from everlasting to everlasting on those who fear [or love] him." In this case, it is not the kind of fear that runs away, but an understanding of worship and love. Those who love God recognize His love as sovereign and fair, unconditional, and eternal. Though we may not always like the consequences that God's correction may bring, we shouldn't doubt what He does is in our best interests. As a good father loves his children and shows compassion and help for them when they are in need or trouble, so does the Lord God do for those who fear (or love) Him.

Day 12

Sing to God, sing praises to his name; lift up a song to
him who rides through the deserts; his name is the Lord;
exult before him! Father of the fatherless and protector of
widows is God in his holy habitation.
—Psalm 68:4–5

I t's easy to say we love God and worship and praise Him, but do we
really understand what worship is? What is praise? Prior to contrary
belief, it is not just singing on Sunday morning. Praise and worship
occur in the depths of the relationship with the Father. Acknowledging
Him as Lord, not just in your words, but in the excitement of who He is.

Worship involves our feelings, our expression of reverence, and our
adoration. It is a time when we focus purely on God and who He is as
Creator, provider, and lover of our souls. The psalmist David, a man after
God's heart, acknowledged God in all He is as our beloved Father. His
songs and worship were wholly heartfelt. God loves our genuineness, so
praise Him for all you are.

Our world is confusing, and the absolutes shunned. Losing sight of
who God is in us grows dimmer. We are so torn with earthly matters that
we must ask ourselves, "Do I know how to love God, and exactly how do
I show that love?" Reintroduce yourself as children of His inheritance and
learn how to worship. Reacquaint yourself with Him. As the Enemy pushes
against us to make other things more important than our relationship with
the Father, we forget that our relationship with Him is a love story written
long before our birth and one that remains faithful and true with God
Almighty. Praise by examining your heart, humbling yourself before Him.
Show your gratitude and adoration. Sing, pray, and walk with Him but fall
in love with the Father again.

Judge not, that you be not judged.
—Matthew 7:1

Superiority. It is the one thing man grasps tightly. No one man is better than the next. Yet man spends a great deal of time sitting in judgment. Jesus tells us not to judge. He doesn't sway from one side to the other. His words are clear. Don't judge. In that phrase, we can dig deeper to see that when we judge others, God spends time bringing our own misgivings to the surface. How can we accuse others when we are sinners ourselves? Our Christian expectations can often lead to a moral and spiritual attitude of superiority. Christ reminds us this is not a path we want to follow. When we point a convicting finger at others without first looking into ourselves, we fail to see our inadequacies.

God sent the Holy Spirit to act as a moral guide, giving us nudges and remorse when we behave less than godly. By that same token, the Holy Spirit serves as our judge by infiltrating those parts of our soul that need refinement. He will give us a spiritual housecleaning and humble us to a point where our pride is squelched. This refinement brings us deeper in Christ. It opens our hearts and minds to the thought that our lives need work daily. We are imperfect and no different than others in our sins of the heart. When you're tempted to judge others, don't let your own sense of Christian superiority raise you above others. You will also be judged in your judgments. Christ died that all people might have forgiveness and an opportunity at a heavenly reward.

Day 14

Beloved, do not be surprised at the fiery trial when it
comes upon you to test you, as though something
strange were happening to you.
—1 Peter 4:12

Christ forewarned those who followed Him that life would be difficult. He suffered great rejection, mockery, and ultimately death, so why should it surprise us, as believers, that our lives would be free of distress and suffering? The difference in our suffering is not any less pain or hurt, but in the fact that as a follower of Christ, we may accept and rejoice in it. Our suffering shows others where our strength is derived. What greater joy than to have a nonbeliever see us experience trials and come out on the other side, wounded but rejoicing. Those who watch wonder, what do they have that I do not? Why can we experience hardships and not be bitter when the unbeliever finds anger and discouragement?

In Christ, we know what is temporal and what is eternal. When we willingly strive for the eternal, the prize is far greater than the suffering. It is simply part of the process. This doesn't mean our pain and sufferings aren't real or valid. No believer would choose to have hardship, and our preference to avoid this is great. We know because Christ has forewarned us that these things will come. As a lover of God, we can accept what may befall us, having the faith to know God will never leave our side and that through our suffering in Christ, others will be changed for the good. Don't be surprised if suffering comes but accept and even rejoice in it as Paul did. Trust in the faithfulness of the Father to bring you through, and you will always find peace.

Week 3—Reassurance That God Is with Us

Faith is difficult. Trusting in something we cannot physically touch or see can be frightening. Still, Hebrews 11:1 teaches us, "Now faith is the assurance of things hoped for, the conviction of things not seen." It is the assurance. The confidence. The promise that what we cannot see or touch is real.

Oddly enough, it seems to be a cycle. You have faith something is real. It proves itself in the waiting. You have faith again, and again it proves itself. Round and round. Over and over. We could say faith is the real test of mankind.

Why do we have faith? What prompts faith in us? Perhaps it's because this is what we're taught. Think back to your childhood when a parent encouraged you to jump into their arms. You mustered up faith to believe that your parent would catch you if you jumped. Maybe it's because we've come to the end of ourselves, and now we reach for something bigger. Sometimes desperation pushes us into blind faith.

Our faith is the assurance of all we hope to be viable and accurate, and in that hope, we find the Father. Our faith grows within that circle in our efforts to develop a relationship with Him. The Father becomes real, and we begin to see His movements. Movements were there, but we did not see them because we had not reached that maturity.

As you study this week, take note of the reassurance that God is alive in you. Grow your faith by reaching deeper into your soul and allowing Him to reside. Take in His promises. Notice how He strengthens you. Take this time to seek the reassurance of God in you.

Day 15

He who dwells in the shelter of the Most High will
abide in the shadow of the Almighty.
—Psalm 91:1

Though we are unsure of the author of this Psalm, Moses is attributed. When we consider all the Israelites had been through and what Moses himself dealt with as he led the people away from Egypt, we have a glimpse of his unfailing faith.

Few can say they genuinely dwell in the shelter of the Most High. Man is sinful and weak and sometimes unable to maintain a clear vision of Christ. They stumble and fall, but to those who remain steadfast, whose faith continues firm, they abide in Him and He in them.

We are a weak sort. Though our intentions are good, our weaknesses seep to the surface. Our nature is to call upon the Almighty when situations grow difficult, just as the children of Israel did in the wilderness. Yet what is hard for us to see clearly, perhaps because of the efforts of the Evil One to thwart us, is that we all might dwell in God's shadow and under His protection. The Father cares for us in ways we cannot see or fathom. His hand of protection extends beyond the width of our shoulders and farther out than we can imagine.

As children of God, as believers, we do not have to be held captive by what we cannot see. We only need to focus on Him and trust that we will be fine under His care. Seeking this type of faith and trust is not easily found. It takes sacred strength and tenacity to see beyond what is earthly and live in what is spiritual—more so, to accept this gift the Father freely offers. Seek a deeper knowledge. Grow your faith. Grasp hold of the spiritual and dwell in the shelter of the Most High. Fully loved and protected. Fully His.

Day 16

The LORD will keep your going out and your
coming in from this time forth and forevermore.
—Psalm 121:8

Psalm 121, as a whole, represented encouragement and affirmation as the children of Israel most likely made their way on a pilgrimage to the temple. As a reminder of God's promise to remain close to His people, these words still hold depth and meaning to the believer. Whether used in private worship or corporate worship as a blessing, there is comfort in knowing the Father is faithful to His children.

When we fall to our knees in submission to Him, we recognize He is the only source of help in our spiritual life. Though God is not held captive by time or space, His skirting across eternity allows Him to step in and out of our lives, physically or spiritually intervening, supporting, and guiding us from His most high place. He is our keeper, provider, and protector, and He knows every step, breath, and moment of our lives. What a comfort to know and believe that we have a God who sees us outwardly and inwardly and one who faithfully stands with us now and forevermore. There is great peace in abiding within the Father, finding reassurance that everything is in His care. Take hold of the peace found in a Father who knows our every breath.

Day 17

For God gave us a spirit not of fear but of
power and love and self-control.
—2 Timothy 1:7

Paul knew his days were ending as he penned this letter to his dear friend Timothy. Paul needed to convey the importance of being bold and strong during this time of impending persecution. He reminded Timothy of his own life and then encouraged him by noting Timothy's personal faith. Rarely has there been a time when Christians could just be comfortable in their faith. Somewhere or somehow, a believer's faith is tested.

Though persecution has not always been physical harm, it has never died away from the earth. The Evil One's goal is to stomp out Christianity, and he fights daily to accomplish that goal. When we undergo hardship, our weaknesses rise. Human nature is for us to turn internally for resolve rather than seeking the Father in His promises and wisdom. Boldness becomes the furthest thing from our minds. Yet Paul instructed Timothy that God gave him a gift of power, love, and self-control—one that came through the Holy Spirit and not from fear.

What an encouragement from Paul when he reminded Timothy, and future believers, that God knew what they would face and He would be near. He provided, well in advance, a spirit for us with power and love rather than fear. As you face trials, embrace the example of Paul's life. Let go of fear and hold to the power, love, and self-control He gives. These are weapons of faith.

Day 18

But they who wait for the LORD shall renew their strength;
they shall mount up with wings like eagles; they shall run
and not be weary; they shall walk and not faint.
—Isaiah 40:31

As a favorite verse of many, this Isaiah scripture touches the hearts of those who struggle. For those who battle sin in their lives or those who think they are strong enough to manage the problems alone—they soon discover they cannot. Perhaps throughout testing, they find their weaknesses are more than they can bear. Isaiah put strong and encouraging words together that everyone could attest to.

Much of our weakness lies in our impatience. We are simply unable to wait on the Lord. His timing and guidance are perfect, yet when we jump ahead of Him and try to rectify or work through a task before the time is right, it isn't long before we find ourselves redoing what could have been easily attained by just waiting on God. God empowers us to fulfill the tasks He gives us. Ponder for a moment—He empowers us to fulfill His plans and work.

Learning to wait on His plan is difficult for us, but the necessary preparation and training for what may lie ahead come within that wait. Remember, God empowers us to fulfill. If we listen and seek after the Father during our time of waiting, our lives begin to reshape. There is no need to repeat a task because we slowly walked, listened, and obeyed. When the time is right, the Father renews our strength. We will mount up with the wings of eagles. We will run and not faint, for God is our everlasting God, Creator, and our mighty and strong tower. Take hold of what is available to us when we wait.

Day 19

The Lord is not slow to fulfill his promise as some count slowness, but is patient toward you, not wishing that any should perish, but that all should reach repentance.

—2 Peter 3:9

Oh, to understand patience, to fully grasp what it means. When the people questioned the return of Christ, when would it happen, they needed to learn to wait. Because God's patience for His return is garnered with desire for as many to return to Him as possible, He patiently waits. It's all in His perfect timing.

The best reply is simply that God is a loving God. His ways are ways that grow us and that wait on us to find our way back. Allowing us to experience difficulties or making us wait is not the Father pointing His finger, smirking, and throwing us into turmoil. The times we enter into are generally situations we are already experiencing. Rather than God heaping more on us, His timing to wait comes into play. By waiting, the child does not get what they want at the moment. Instead, they learn to maneuver their way back. Hopefully, their trust boosts. Those bold in their faith have learned not to fear understanding patience.

We are far too impatient when we ask God for provision or help. We desire that He answer immediately and give us what we need. Still, in His timing, God is slow and precise in His answers. He knows what lies ahead, and He understands rushing is not in our best interests. The Father longs for us all to abide in Him. His ways are designed to lead us to depend on Him, not drive us away. He waits patiently for every child to return to Him, for His heart breaks at the loss of even one. Patience is merely learning to wait. While you wait, soak in the refining power of the Father. Learn from it. Seek it. He will never forsake you.

Day 20

The heart is deceitful above all things, and desperately sick; who can understand it? "I the LORD search the heart and test the mind, to give every man according to his ways, according to the fruit of his deeds."
—Jeremiah 17:9–10

The word *heart* has lost its deeper meaning thanks to commercialism. We loosely use *heart* as a simple sign of love, and though there is nothing wrong with that, we miss the more significant meaning by not looking deeper. In Jeremiah's passage, "heart" referred to the center of man's emotion. It included the mind, emotion, and man's will. The heart was the very essence of man.

When our hearts fill with deceit and sin, the man's soul is also filled with deceit. But when a man has a pure heart, then so is the man. Jeremiah called out the people for their lustful and deceitful ways. Their hearts (minds and souls) were anything but holy, godly, or pure. They couldn't see their sin. Often we fail to recognize the sin in our lives. A failure to acknowledge our sin means we see no wrong in what we do nor a need to bring our lives back into harmony with the Father.

Psalm 51 cries out to God to, "Wash me thoroughly from my iniquity, and cleanse me from my sin! Create in me a clean heart . . . renew a right spirit within me."

Examine your heart—the center of all emotion. Remove the postage stamp idea of what heart means. A solid relationship with the Father allows us to look into ourselves, see what needs to change, and make an effort to rectify. The Father already sees deep into our souls, deep into our hearts. We cannot hide from Him, nor can we hide our sin. Seek after Him and let Him cleanse you fully.

Day 21

For I am sure that neither death nor life, nor angels nor rulers,
nor things present nor things to come, nor powers, nor height
nor depth, nor anything else in all creation, will be able to
separate us from the love of God in Christ Jesus our Lord.
—Romans 8:38–39

Who of us can truly grasp the immenseness of God? In all His glory, He is greater than anything we can imagine. Paul issued several challenges to anything that might influence or thwart the church in Rome just before He shared this. Earlier, Paul said there would be no condemnation, and now he concludes with this reminder. No separation. What a beautiful statement of God's mighty love for the believer. It is, in essence, an eternal security reminder. By Paul stating the negative, *neither* and *nor* make a strong impact throughout these two verses. "Neither death nor life, nor angels nor rulers, . . . nor height nor depth, nor anything else in all creation, will be able to separate us." This phrasing alone proves Paul's determination to show us God's faithfulness.

There is no greater reminder in times of joy and hardship than this. God is always with us. Even when we falter or stray, His love does not change. We are still His children, His creations. Still, a glory to Him, and still, He calls us His own.

The issue for man is that we suffer from a lack of belief. When things do not go our way, our faith dwindles. We question if God loves us—even after we've experienced fantastic provision or grace. God offers His love freely, and nothing will be able to separate us from that love. His love is the greatest gift man could have. Reach to Him. Remember, nothing can separate you from His love. Lean close into the arms of the Savior and find rest and comfort.

Week 4—Hope in God's Faithfulness

No hope. This seems to be the world's mantra. It's an easy mantra to follow. Just look at the state of the world—discord, hate, anger, violence. There seems to be no hope. When Gallup, a global analytics and advice firm, asked teens in an October 2000 Gallup Youth Survey who their heroes were, a staggering number stated (out of the five hundred teens polled) no one. No one to look up to, no one to call a hero, in essence, no one to emulate.[1]

As we consider these statistics from a Christian worldview, we see that one of the most vital age groups of those who are our future has little to no direction. When all they see is violence and anger, how can they know there is hope? When they literally do not know who Christ is, other than He is a person like Gandhi or Abraham Lincoln, then there is no hope. In a world of no hope, there is no future.

Instilling the absolutes of a Christian worldview begin within the confines of our own beliefs. What do you believe, and more so, do you really believe it? It's easy to say God is faithful but stepping onto faith and believing this can be trying.

We are called to make disciples, to go into the world and preach and teach, but unless we know what we believe—unless we believe in the principles of God, we are not primed for spiritual success. It begins with us.

As you study this week, seek out the faithfulness of God. Make a note to be intentional about giving thanks. Believe that what God has said will never pass away. Know there is salvation and that God is exactly who He says He is.

Strengthen your hope, and through that, God can and will open significant avenues for understanding and action.

Day 22

And you will say in that day: "Give thanks to the LORD,
call upon his name, make known his deeds among the peoples,
proclaim that his name is exalted."
—Isaiah 12:4

Even in God's anger with His people, He gives mercy. Never forget that those God has reconciled Himself to, He comforts. God was angry with His children during the time of Isaiah, yet even in His frustration and anger, He guided Isaiah with instructions and warnings for the people. The Father may have stepped back, but He never walked away—proof of His unfailing love for His people.

Giving thanks to the Lord is sometimes difficult, especially when we face trials where we see no end, but in this case, the worshipper is so filled with thanksgiving that he cannot contain his excitement. The people were in a difficult season with the Father. Their disobedience grieved Him. Still, He offered "wells of salvation" (v. 3)—wells of salvation that could be drawn from by the bucketful.

Our thankfulness means so much to God, for He sees our love through it. His hope and our hope continues that man will return to their place with Him. Learning to praise His name in times of hardship leads us to hope in what seems to be a hopeless situation, and it reminds us of the many good and wonderful things God has done for us before this difficulty.

Praise His name. Exalt Him. Let others know of the joys and provisions the Almighty has done for you in the past, then accept that more is to come. He will not forsake you. He may discipline you, but the Lord God has reconciled His people to Himself. He will never walk away.

Day 23

Heaven and earth will pass away, but my
words will not pass away.
—Matthew 24:35

None of us wants to see the world end. It seems impossible, and there would undoubtedly be no joy in Armageddon. The loss is too much to consider—our families, friends, and all we love. As mankind, we have difficulty looking beyond what we physically know.

Christ spent vast amounts of time teaching those who followed Him with parables, those simple stories related to current situations and times that people in that day could understand. He used these stories to teach the multitude, but He used them equally to teach His disciples. These men loved Jesus so much and wanted desperately to understand all He said, but at times they too had difficulty seeing beyond what was physical. The things Jesus taught—the value of love, forgiveness, peace, and how to treat others—were so different than the law they were raised to know. Sometimes these things were the polar opposite of the laws the disciples knew. This was their first introduction to the eternal life Christ prepared them for, and at times it seemed mind-boggling.

Jesus used the parable of the fig tree to help them understand that the tree was planted, bloomed its leaves and fruit for a time, and then ended. So would this world, but what would never end was God and His words, His power, and the place He deemed as eternity. Our world is challenging and though we cannot imagine its demise, what we must look forward to is eternity. Forever with the Father. God is the Alpha and Omega, and the creation of this world fits that same pattern—a beginning and an end, but what never ends is the promise and the reward of glory with God the Father. That transcends everything.

Day 24

Behold, God is my salvation; I will trust, and will
not be afraid; for the Lord God is my strength
and my song, and he has become my salvation.
—Isaiah 12:2

At long last. A song of praise for the people of Israel. God's anger
burned against them for their blatant sin. He worked through
Isaiah to send both warnings and hope that His love was still
genuine even though He was angry. Isaiah wanted the people to return to
the feet of the Father, and his words of praise served as encouragement.
Despite their failings, he still found hope in God.

Just as Isaiah did, we can find hope in God when things look bleak.
When many choose other life verses, this one stands out as promise and
encouragement. Our salvation is entirely in the hands of the Savior, and
it's up to us to trust in Him—to believe Him. It's often been said, "You
say you believe, but the question is, do you really believe? Do you believe
God will and has already done all He has promised He would do?"

Learning to trust is trying for a people who easily grow impatient
with God's timing. We quickly fall to our knees to call out to the Father,
but we are unwilling to wait on His movement. Instead, we take things
into our own hands.

The gifts we receive from the Father are immense and bountiful.
However, we have difficulty accepting the gift of His strength. The
strength of God lives in us. Did you hear that? The strength of God *in us*.
There is no need to fear when we accept this strength that abides within
us. In fact, fear is almost nil, and we are open to His salvation. Sing to
God a new song of praise for our salvation is in Him. Our hope is in Him.
His love is in us.

> But Ruth said, "Do not urge me to leave you or to
> return from following you. For where you go I will go,
> and where you lodge I will lodge. Your people shall
> be my people, and your God my God."
> —Ruth 1:16

The loyalty of Ruth to Naomi is heartwarming. She could remarry among her own people, find a life, and start over. Yet, she remained with her mother-in-law. This speaks to two things: first, the love Ruth felt for Naomi. She didn't want Naomi to be left alone with no one to care for her. And second, it speaks to her sense of faithfulness and loyalty to family.

When we look at what loyalty is, we find its meaning as steadfast, unmovable, and sturdy. Those three words speak volumes when we first look at the dedication of Ruth to her mother-in-law and her dead husband. When we apply them to our heavenly Father, it becomes a true wow factor.

Ruth could have walked away. She could have started over under the care of her family in her own land, but she chose a life of uncertainty to remain with Naomi. Our Father never decides to walk away. He promised that He would not leave us or forsake us. Walking away has never been an option for God. When we ignore His faithfulness to us, He steps one step to the side so that we can choose the path we wish to follow. Once our decision is made, He takes that step back and remains directly behind us. Never budging. Never leaving. Never deserting. Our God is faithful. Though our human minds sometimes demand the tangible over faith, He still steps back into place behind us, waiting for us to turn around and run back into His arms. God is faithful. Turn around and be welcomed into His loving arms.

Day 26

For in him the whole fullness of deity dwells bodily,
and you have been filled in him, who is the
head of all rule and authority.
—Colossians 2:9–10

Man is easily deceived. Easily swayed. The cause is that man's understanding leans on what they see with their eyes rather than on the faith they carry within. When our beliefs are based on sight, it is easy to assume that belief in Christ is difficult simply because we, those who came after Christ's death, do not physically see Him. Following those who offer promises that better suit our needs is much easier than adhering to the principles of God. After all, we want what we want, not necessarily what Christ wants.

Paul warned the people of Colossae to hold tightly to Christ. Do not be swayed by the false teachings of others. Christ carried the whole (fullness) of the Father in Him. Through Christ, we can experience all that God is, and we can know Him fully. The promise of our completeness in Christ and the Father came to us through His sacrifice.

As the world pushes more and more to rule away absolutes as we know them, the temptation to know Christ grows smaller. Still, nothing changes with the Father. He is still the Creator, Savior, and King, the head of all principality and power.

When life pushes strings of unbelief toward you, grasp hold of what is permanent. Wrap yourself in the experience and love of God, and do not be misled, for He is still ruler and King of all whose love for you extends far greater than you can conceive.

Day 27

We destroy arguments and every lofty opinion raised
against the knowledge of God, and take every
thought captive to obey Christ.
—2 Corinthians 10:5

I f every thought, every motive, idea, or desire is taken captive, then the whole of us belongs to Christ. Do not be deceived otherwise as the world pitches its agenda, doing its best to reclaim the very whole of us from Christ. Despite what others try to lead us to believe, God does not loosen His hold on those He calls His own.

We cannot depend on the knowledge or wisdom of others for our spiritual safety. That safety lies in exposing and defeating those thoughts that might lead to placing anything or anyone else in God's supreme spot. It is we who must remain faithful and prayerful. We who must search inwardly to find and take captive those thoughts that claw at who Christ is.

This brings our hearts and thoughts directly into line with Christ Jesus and gives them all over in obedience to the Father. Can we be expected to stop every enemy that attacks the spiritual safety we seek? No, but when we come into obedience with our minds and hearts, God's love and care scoops us into Him. The more we spend time thinking about Christ, incorporating Him into our hearts, the less room there is for temptation and deception. The more we can capture and destroy those things that seek to tear Him down.

Look inward. Seek out those thoughts and desires that bring corruption into your soul. Capture them and destroy them so that you might live fully in Him.

Day 28

Fear not, for I am with you; be not dismayed, for
I am your God; I will strengthen you, I will help you,
I will uphold you with my righteous right hand.
—Isaiah 41:10

God is not the originator of fear. He is the defeater of fear, but He knows as humans, the fear the Evil One pushes to instill in us can be convincing and overwhelming. Yet He, the God of all that is fearless, reminds us over three hundred times throughout Scripture to fear not. "Do not be afraid" and "Be of good courage" are not idle words. Instead, they offer strong hope to us as believers who hold on amid our fear.

God reassured His people through Isaiah that they should not worry or fear. He is God, there to strengthen and help them. He was and still remains faithful to His people. God has never steered away from His children, even in His rightful frustration or anger with Israel. Like a parent teaching their toddler to obey, there were times God stepped to the side to allow His people to experience the consequences of their disobedience, but because of His deep love, He can and does not ever forsake His children. God is a loving Father, poised to stretch out a hand at any point.

He is not a god who rules by fear, rather one who guides us *through* the fear of our consequences. God is not a father who sets His children on their way, refusing to warn them of obstacles that lay ahead. He is a faithful Father who offers us wisdom, strength, and ability.

When worry and fear smother you, stretch your arms upward and breathe in the life and promises of God.

Week 5—Belief God Is
Who He Says He Is

We are a people who rely on sight. If we don't see it, we often don't believe it. Many times, it's due to a lack of trust. Sometimes a fear in the unknown. Whatever roadblock deters our belief, we depend on what we see with our eyes to make most determinations, and our first step to knowing Christ better is believing in what we *do not* see.

There is reassurance in what we can touch, and when we lose sight of what is tangible, we are sure to fall into fear. Coming to know Christ brings us a solid reassurance that He is real. Even the world around us shouts of His presence—from the trees to every animal that crawls on the earth. He is real, and He is who He says He is. When we heed the peace and presence of Christ, both spiritually and physically, it strengthens the foundations of our faith.

Life without a compass is scary, and when our trust is in Him, then our pocket holds a compass that will not steer us wrong. We must learn to use the compass to know how to turn and find our way onto the path of righteousness. Sometimes we might grow a little cocky and veer off in a direction that looks safe, a shortcut. Still, we are reminded that "strait is the gate, and narrow is the way." And so, we tilt our compasses and allow them to right themselves, stepping again into the path of faith and the belief that God has promised to be with us. We believe He is strong, wise, and faithful. We believe He will not fail us. Simply put, we believe God is who He says He is.

Spend time in prayer this week. Seek out what you need that helps you believe fully in the Master. God has promised, "seek, and you will find."

Day 29

If possible, so far as it depends on you, live peaceably with all.
—Romans 12:18

The adage "history repeats itself" is most certainly true as we read Romans. Paul's letter to the church mimics life today. He fired off one exhortation after the other: love one another, live in harmony, don't be haughty, associate with the lowly, don't be cocky, and never avenge. Paul kindly but effectively laid out the issues he saw.

Twice he reminded the church to live in harmony, live peaceably, a cursor to the issues they faced and a mirror to our world today. As we watch media today smear the worst of humanity before our eyes, there seems to be nothing but unrest, deceit, and hate—even among the brotherhood of Christians. Man has long been divided by their own beliefs, never willing to bend so that we can come together as one church of believers under the headship of our Lord and King rather than as a group of denominations. It has always been the desire of mankind to be right rather than submissive. When we see the mayhem happening in our world today, our thought is to lean back and shout, "Why can't we all just love one another?"

That, in and of itself, is the question. More than once, Scripture addresses the need for unity. More than once we are reminded by Jesus to love one another. Yet, in our arrogance, we cannot let go of our selfishness long enough to embrace or reap the rewards of obedience to that one simple command. Love your neighbor.

It is difficult to live peaceably in a world filled with chaos, but as Christians, Paul is reminding us, this is not an option. Simply put, it is what we must do. When we follow in obedience to live peaceably, amazing things happen. If you are in a place where you must choose to live at peace or in chaos, isn't the answer obvious?

Day 30

For with the heart one believes and is justified, and with
the mouth one confesses and is saved. So faith comes from
hearing, and hearing through the Word of Christ.
—Romans 10:10, 17

Getting our heads around the love of God is challenging. It was especially challenging for the Jews during Paul's time. Imagine their confusion. Years of living strictly by the law and then Christ entered the picture, presenting a new relational way to know the Father. In fairness, it had to be difficult making a complete turnaround from what they knew to what Jesus, and Paul after Him, was teaching. It was an equally taxing job for Paul to convince the Jews differently.

In Scripture, we see Paul's frustration boil, but these verses tend to read with genuine compassion and desire for him to find a way to help the people understand their beliefs. He described it beautifully and simplistically. When the heart believes, there is justification. When the mouth confesses, there is salvation. That happens by hearing the Word of Christ.

We must hear. Grasp hold. Confess. Then there is salvation. Once these words penetrate the heart, our lives change. The walk and the relationship take on a new premise. Our pathway to heaven is not simply in the good we do but in the belief and faith that we house within our hearts. The process is threefold. Hear, confess, accept.

Only God could conceive such a simple plan for understanding. If you question your relationship with Christ, go back to the Word. Enter in. Absorb. Hear. Confess. Accept. Reaffirm your faith.

Day 31

Now faith is the assurance of things hoped for,
the conviction of things not seen.
—Hebrews 11:1

Dr. Charles Stanley beautifully described the degrees of faith. He explained *little faith* is hoping God will do what He says He will. *Great faith* is knowing God will do what He has said He would do. *Perfect faith* is knowing that God has already done what He said He would do.

Faith is a tedious thing. We seem to innately understand its meaning. Yet when we try to define it, we are at a loss for words. Faith. The belief in what we cannot see seems especially hard. We are a people who depend on sight. If we cannot see it, then it is not true.

The writer of Hebrews did his best to help the Hebrew people understand faith. He began his explanation by noting that we know the universe was created by the Word of God, telling the people, "what is seen was not made out of things that are visible" (v. 3).

Faith hinges on our focus. When we can fully focus on God and honestly believe what He promises and tells us, then our faith strengthens. No man or woman is perfect, but does that mean we can never achieve perfect faith? Maybe not perfect, but close. The more our faith matures, the greater is our belief in the God who rules the universe. In the situations we face, our faith may slip through all the phases of faith. Yet, as the maturing Christian, we don't tarry long on *little faith*.

A relationship built on faith is complex. When we rest our faith in Christ, our growth in Him manifests itself as deep and abiding love. When your faith waivers, remember the assurances we are promised and strive for perfect faith, knowing God has already done what He promised.

Therefore, since we are surrounded by so great a cloud of witnesses,
let us also lay aside every weight, and sin which clings so closely,
and let us run with endurance the race that is set before us, looking
to Jesus, the founder and perfecter of our faith, who for the joy that
was set before him endured the cross, despising the shame, and is
seated at the right hand of the throne of God.
—Hebrews 12:1–2

What better analogy than that of a race to describe pushing through hardship. The writer of Hebrews used the same type of example, but he wasn't necessarily going through a problem. Instead, his encouragement was to push through life, not as a sprint. Instead as a marathon. A long-haul race. He so longed for the people to understand what it meant to labor through this life and have the assurance when the race was complete, the reward was not necessarily in the trophy but in finishing the race with the endurance (or faith) built through a deeper relationship with Christ.

Our humanity loves the things that bring us joy, and we are inclined to overindulge. Paul is, however, saying to the people to lay aside every weight and sin that ensnares them. When we take time to think of those weights, they may not all be sin. They may, instead, be those things we overindulge in, those things we put ahead of Christ. Look at the Olympic marathon runner. They dress light, grab water as they run, open their mouth wide, sloshing in one gulp, and pour the remainder over their bodies. Then they toss off the weight of the bottle, flinging it to the side. Anything additional weighs them down. So it should be for us. In a relationship working toward heaven—dress light. There is a great cloud of witnesses cheering for us. Throw off any excess weight because winning the race is fine. Finishing is far better.

Day 33

I press on toward the goal for the prize of the
upward call of God in Christ Jesus.
—Philippians 3:14

The trophy is the prize gained by the winner. There is generally only one first-place winner. Only one who takes home the real prize, but that is not true in the life of the Christian. There is no trophy in first place. Instead, all who press toward the goal and *finish* receive the award—eternal life.

We are a blessed people. Before He knit us together in our mother's secret place, He'd already chosen who we were from the color of our eyes to our gifts and talents. When God created us, He left a small void within us that only He could fill. Only His presence can suffice. His call to us is tucked away in that spot, waiting to emerge. When we strive to better this relationship with the Father, to know Him intimately, that call rises. We are encouraged to press closer to Him and stretch further to grasp hold.

With each stride forward, the prize becomes clearer. It takes demanding work, strife, and hardships to strengthen us. Why is attaining it so hard if God calls us toward Him? Shouldn't we just be given this? We are promised the prize at the end of the race—to finish victoriously in Him if we have served and loved Him well, but from man's fall, sin entered in, and those are the hurdles we must clear. Our promise was never that it would be easy attainment but that the prize of eternity waits for those who press toward the goal and finish the race. What a call. What a gift.

A trophy for one winner is nice, but a prize for all who jump the hurdles, for all who finish successfully, even when their legs ache, brings a greater gain—eternal life. It's a prize we can all have. The call is there, the work tedious, but the payout is eternal.

Day 34

But be doers of the word, and not hearers only,
deceiving yourselves.
—James 1:22

A young child goes to school not just to learn to read and write but also to navigate the world as they know it. Children not only hear and learn to read words, but they use those words in everything. They, in essence, become doers with their words.

James spent a focused amount of time teaching the importance of being a doer of the Word. Just to know God's Word is not enough. Simply being a part of it, again, is not enough. Once we are armed with His words, we must become individuals who don't sit idle. Instead, we come to our feet and live the Word. Knowing and understanding the Word gives us cause to live differently, to no longer live in what we once knew but to step into the righteousness of God and live as Christ.

We are recognized not by the things we know but by what we do. Those are the lasting things. Everything we do will influence someone. The question becomes, how do you want to use your influence? What will others see in you that makes them desire Christ?

Our determination to live as Christ makes a difference, even when we cannot see the indention on the world. There is no eternal benefit in knowing the Word and doing nothing with it. When we become doers, our lives are used, and our sights are set toward heaven, shining for all to see. Do not hear and walk away. Hear, apply to your life, and then do.

Are not five sparrows sold for two pennies? And not one of them
is forgotten before God. Why, even the hairs of your head are all
numbered. Fear not; you are of more value than many sparrows.
—Luke 12:6–7

Never question your value in God's eyes. The Evil One seeks to tear
us down mentally. We look for the physical attacks, almost expect
them, but our eyes are blinded to the mental attacks that rain
down on us for one reason or another. Satan works, not from the standpoint
of our strengths, for he cannot compare to them, but he needles his way
into our minds through our weaknesses. Attacking our self-confidence is
easy because, as humans, our mental well-being is vulnerable. We become
easy targets when we question our self-worth to our Father and our friends.

Jesus seemed burdened by the worry of those He preached to in this
passage. He recognized their fear. It was a tumultuous time for believers.
His reassurance to the people was not a promise that things would be easy
but rather a reminder of whom the people should fear and be dependent
upon. Picture the gentleness of the Savior as He walked among the people.
Take in His desire to calm the fear, and grasp hold of the reassurance He
gave that day. What good is it to fear one who can simply take your life
but do nothing else? Fear the one who can cast you into hell. Don't worry.
God knows every part of you. If He finds value in the sparrows, imagine
how much more value He sees in you.

The Father loves His children, and though we know this as believers,
we tend to lose sight of how He cares for us. He doesn't want to lose one
soul. God allows us the freedom to choose to love Him. His love for us is
strong, and our value in His eyes is beyond our understanding.

Week 6—The Truth of His Ways

"**O**h, what a tangled web we weave, when we choose to deceive." There couldn't be a better Shakespearean phrase for us to adhere to, except that this phrase is *not* from Shakespeare. Sir Walter Scott penned the words in 1808, and the quote is *incorrect*. It should read, "Oh, what a tangled web we weave, when first we practice to deceive."

This is a perfect example of how our Christian worldview becomes skewed. It may begin as a misquoted writer, but even the quote becomes watered down and the translation muddied as time passes. It seems trivial since it's just a mistake, but it leads to a deeper conundrum. Individuals fail to *know* what they believe, and worse, they believe what they are told without question.

No longer do individuals seek truth in what they see and hear. If it sounds right, then it probably is, or at least this is what our world has led us to believe. The loss of our Christian worldview hasn't happened in big chunks. It's in the deletion of a word, inching in the wrong so slowly and intentionally that suddenly the wrong looks right. And no one questions it.

During this next week of devotions, pay attention to how even Paul's words were twisted. Take note of those whom he praised for their steadfastness to the Word and apply the importance of praying, studying, and seeking the good in others. Take time to look over your beliefs and your actions. What do you participate in, and what have you grown to justify that years ago, you would not? Readjust your thoughts. Pay attention to the world around you and be different. Be fruitful by His standards. Take in His Word and make it a living part of your life. This is how we begin to reestablish our Christian worldview. It's not in complaining or shaking our heads in disapproval. It is in knowing the Word of God and allowing it to be front and center in everything we do. Every action. Every mindset. Every word. All of these begin with us. Won't you start now?

Day 36

We give thanks to God always for all of you,
constantly mentioning you in our prayers, remembering before
our God and Father your work of faith and labor of love and
steadfastness of hope in our Lord Jesus Christ.
—1 Thessalonians 1:2–3

Standing firm in our convictions, steadfastness, and a deep devotion to the cause of Christ aren't easy feats—not when the world pushes hard for us to concede and reconcile to its beliefs. Chaos demands our attention, forcing out the ease of standing firm in our principles. The Thessalonians, though not perfect, held strong and firm in their convictions to Christ.

Paul noted at the beginning of his book to the church at Thessalonica that he constantly prayed for them. They remembered the strong faith, labors of love, and steadfastness that these believers held in a time of hardship. He was thankful for the people's devotion, especially when the church was young and faced great difficulty there. Paul found great encouragement in the faith and steadfastness of these people to the cause of Christ. Nothing encourages more than seeing the fruit of your labor remain strong and fulfilled. The seed Paul planted formed strong roots, leading to a strong church.

Our convictions mean something. They stand out to those who surround us. The difficulty comes when we are tested. Are we able to shine the light of Christ? Choose beliefs with meaning and power rather than the newest flag-waving trends. Stand firm.

I went up because of a revelation and set before them
(though privately before those who seemed influential) the
gospel that I proclaim among the Gentiles, in order to make
sure I was not running or had not run in vain.
—Galatians 2:2

The work we do is important, whether it be our efforts to make a living or help with projects. When we invest our hearts into a project, it means something to see its success. One small doubt can tear down a hard-worked effort.

Paul hit a snag in his ministry. Naysayers, passing themselves off as "representatives or leaders" in the church, set out to undermine the work of his ministry. At a time when an infant church was gaining ground, some came behind the true teaching (inspired to Paul by Jesus), planting doubt and confusion. Their questions regarding the old law versus the new covenant were just enough to instill confusion and doubt. Paul wasted no time talking with the church leaders in Galatia to clarify and validate his teachings were true.

When we work to accomplish a task, but circumstance places doubt, it is easy to feel our work was a waste. Paul was frustrated at the undermining ways of the few, and though he seemed to wonder if the work was a waste, he quickly thwarted the thought by taking action to rectify the confusion.

The efforts and desire to know the Father are right and good. Remain tight in the Word, for there lies the only truth. Christ's sacrifice for you was not in vain and neither is your belief of the Father. Be steadfast and firm and others will see your unfaltering love of God.

Day 38

See that no one repays anyone evil for evil, but
always seek to do good to one another and to everyone.
—1 Thessalonians 5:15

Getting even. These ideas are what the world shoves at us daily: "What I have is mine, and no one has the right to touch it." Life seems filled with nothing but selfishness and disregard for others. People puff their chests and demand equality, even if that means returning anger for anger. Hurt for hurt. It's easy to get swept into the turmoil that the Evil One stirs. He makes it seem logical and right to return the fire. Injustice after injustice only brings about scorn and hate.

Paul addressed several things to the Thessalonian church that were good and right and a reminder of goodwill and common sense. Don't seek to get even. It only breeds animosity and anger. Instead, be different. Search for the good in others.

Searching for the good amid the bad can be trying and frustrating. There's always that *one* person who grates against our last nerve. However, there is good even in the vilest. The challenge for us is seeking that out. Does our finding it mean that it will change that person? Unfortunately, no, but it changes us, and that is a far more incredible accomplishment for our spiritual well-being. Seeking the good in the worst gives us a new perspective. It allows us to view others through the eyes that have changed us. When we see through the eyes of love, it lasers through the hard exterior of the ones whom we detest and gives us compassion. After all, God looks for the good in our sinfulness.

Do good, even when it seems impossible. Remember Christ as He took blow after blow of torture. "Father, forgive them."

Day 39

I have no greater joy than to hear that
my children are walking in the truth.
—3 John 1:4

Very few rush to tell us the good things about our children. Instead, it's the opposite. If there is an issue, others race to inform us of the misdeeds of our offspring. According to what others say, we often wonder if our children do anything other than rabble-rousing. Has our parenting been in vain, a worthless effort that has only managed to produce unruly children? Of course not, but man's negativity leans first to what is wrong as opposed to that which is right. Perhaps this is a foothold of the Evil One, a way he can instill chaos and frustration into our hearts.

John immediately offered a compliment in this letter to Gaius, a traveling companion, a fellow believer, and a respected teacher. He shared that he had no greater joy than hearing his children walked in the truth. What a pleasing compliment to both John and Gaius. The work they'd done with those they instructed in the Word and the love of Christ remained staunch in their beliefs. During this time, John, like Paul, was spending time correcting the body of Christ. Some were misled by men who chose to interject false teachings. It was a breath of fresh air for John to see the work they had done remained strong under the guidance of Gaius.

Others often try to stifle the joy we have in Christ by pointing out the most minute failures. Do not dismay. Hold firm to the purity of Christ. Remain in His Word and pray for His guidance in your understanding. The Father is joyful at your faithfulness.

Day 40

God spoke to our fathers by the prophets, but in
these last days he has spoken to us by his Son,
whom he appointed the heir of all things.
—Hebrews 1:1–4

Who is Jesus? The easy answer: the Son of God. A correct answer for a believer. But what if you were born Jewish in the days of Jesus? What if your upbringing was to believe a different idea about the Messiah to come? The question might still loom.

The writer of Hebrews doesn't introduce himself as in most letters; instead, he launches directly into answering the question of the supremacy of Jesus. He is quick to remind the people that before Jesus, *God spoke through prophets, but now He has spoken through His Son, the heir.* The writer boldly says Jesus "is the radiance of the glory of God and the exact imprint of his nature." He wastes no time giving Jesus the proper place in the Trinity.

It is no secret that the ministry of Jesus was different than what the Jewish people understood. They lived by the law, and now this new side of God was shocking and changed. Jesus spoke of love, gentleness, kindness, peace, and other attributes of God the people were unaccustomed to seeing. His was a challenging ministry, to guide the people from what they knew to what their worship of God could be. The writer clearly states who Jesus is. "He upholds the universe by the word of his power." He purified us and took His place at the right hand of God.

If you question who Jesus is, remember to look toward the glory of Jesus. Focus on the hope, joy, and life found only through an unchanging God.

Day 41

Know this, my beloved brothers: let every person be quick to hear,
slow to speak, slow to anger; for the anger of man does
not produce the righteousness of God.
—James 1:19–20

A bridled tongue is hard to come by in this day and time. Anger rises at the drop of a hat, and few take the time to listen. Everyone is right in their own opinion, and few are willing to concede. Before we can complete a sentence, others have finished it, taking the words and twisting them. Inflaming emotions. Tearing down communications and relationships. It's a quick anger.

James takes time to instruct the people that a wave of uncontrolled anger leads to flaming words that do not produce the righteousness of God. His usage of the word *righteousness* is similar to the usage seen in the Old Testament, doing what God has required His people to do. This is the same thing that Jesus taught and did, living our lives according to the will of God and not clasping tightly to our own wills.

Our world suffers, and amid anguish and challenges, it is easy for our hearing to deafen and our words to explode. It seems to be an almost natural human response to hardship, but James implores every person to strive to control their actions and words. Each of us can successfully manage this when we place those emotions into the hands of the Father. "Let the words of my mouth and the meditation of my heart be acceptable in your sight" (Psalm 19:14). May they bring glory to God and transformation in us. On our own, we cannot attain such control. Only in God is hope found. Only through God is this possible.

Day 42

Now to him who is able to keep you from stumbling and
to present you blameless before the presence of his glory
with great joy . . . be glory, majesty, dominion, and authority.
—Jude 24–25

Praise and blessing. Often, we are void of either in a sinful world. We find ourselves struggling against the powers of evil, pushing us away from doing the primary things God created us to do—praise and worship.

It's been said God is a vain deity, demanding His followers praise Him for His good works. How self-centered can a god be? As Christians, we know that is not true. Though God demands His rightful place, He is the furthest thing from vain possible. So how do we defend a God who inhabits (enthroned on) the praise of His people? He wants us to praise Him because He knows what it will do for and in us. We align ourselves with His purposes, ways, perspectives, and holiness as we praise Him. Those aspects of our lives that are misaligned become realigned when we worship.

Jude reminds the people that it is God who keeps them from falling. He is great and mighty in authority. As Creator of all that is, God is the great *I Am*. He is worthy of all praise, glory, and worship. Through His loving kindness and mercy, He has earned and deserves the praise of His people, for lack of better words. Praise is a recognition of His greatness. More so, a testimony to His faithfulness, His provision, and His care. God is mighty in His authority and His Majesty. By His power to save us, He is still available to us. He will one day bring us home to live with Him eternally. Praise Him for who He is and for His love for you.

Week 7—Praise Strengthens Our Relationship with the Father

Most folks enjoy Sunday morning praise, whether it is filled with old hymns, new praise songs, or a good combination of both. It is crucial to remain pure within the confines of our praise. Praise songs can bring us to high emotion with words that prick our hearts and open a floodgate of tears. Though there is nothing wrong with being invested and blessed by our singing of praises, it is vital to remember what the praise is for and, more so, for whom it is meant. Where has our heart traveled when our praise wanes away from God and hangs in the emotion?

Just a word of warning, do not read into this what is not there. Praise and worship should offer us joy and even transform our hearts as a people, but we cannot lose sight that our praise is offered for the Father.

Psalm 22:3 (KJV) says, "O thou that inhabitest the praises of Israel." God loves our praise, and our churches today are blessed with singers and songwriters who can convey lyrics that touch the soul, for He inhabits the praises of His people.

As you draw closer to Him this week, praise Him for He is good. Praise Him as you love Him, with all your soul, heart, and mind. Do not allow yourself to redirect praise that should be centered toward the Father toward yourself. Remain focused on the heart of God. Enjoy the praise. Worship to the fullest, and when you do, the Father will take it in as sweet incense, and you, too, will be blessed.

Day 43

Do not be afraid and do not be dismayed at this great
horde, for the battle is not yours but God's.
—2 Chronicles 20:15

We like to fight our own battles. Though we may drop to our knees momentarily and plead to God for help, it is not long before we take matters into our own hands. Whether it's stubbornness or impatience because God does not move when we expect, it comes down to the fact that we like to fight our own battles. No one can defend us better than ourselves.

King Jehoshaphat and the children of Israel faced an attack from three sides. Doom seemed to be imminent. Though Jehoshaphat was not the perfect King, he brought the people together and prayed as a nation for God's mercy. God heard and conveyed the message that assured them the battle was not theirs to fight. When the Israelites arrived for battle, the enemy was laid to waste, having fought one another. The battle was God's.

Jehoshaphat called together all the people, and they lifted their hands in prayer. There is great power in prayer. When God's people pray together, they are strengthened. God responds. Imagine, if our nation came together, laid our differences and opinions to the side, and prayed. What would happen? From the depths of all eternity, God would rise up and take the battle as His own. And He would prevail.

Prayer, in any form, is mighty, for God hears every cry and takes on every battle, and then fights them according to His will. Do not fight your battles alone, for the battle is His.

Day 44

Oh come, let us worship and bow down; let us kneel
before the LORD, our Maker! For he is our God, and
we are the people of his pasture, and the sheep of his hand.
—Psalm 95:6–7

I t's nice to belong. To find a spot, a group, a trusted friend, where we fit perfectly and personalities agree. The understanding of the world as we see it makes sense and rings in harmony. Humans need to feel as though they belong.

In the Psalms he wrote, David often used the analogy and situations he faced daily as a shepherd caring for his sheep. He noted throughout his writings how his sheep knew his voice, looked to him for safety, and trusted him. Without a doubt, this shepherd conveyed that his sheep belonged.

The sweetest of the Psalms reminds us that we are the sheep of our Shepherd, God. David poured out his personal love, adoration, and faults before a loving God he believed and who he knew cared deeply for him.

We see the joy he finds in worship and prayer in his praise. Imagine him whirling around, staff in the air, singing praises. When we read his laments, we feel his most profound sorrow pushed to the feet of God so that he finds much needed comfort and rest. This psalmist, this writer, this shepherd, felt as though he belonged solely to God. He found peace and was lifted up when he worshipped and praised. He belonged. Offering glory to the Great Shepherd was easy because he felt he belonged. When you feel as though you are alone, bury yourself in the Psalms. Allow yourself to be a part of a flock, cared for, and well loved. You will belong.

Day 45

Then he said to them, "But who do you say that I am?"
And Peter answered, "The Christ of God."
—Luke 9:18–20

I f ever there was a convicting question, it would be Jesus asking His disciples, "But who do you say that I am?" It's a question that, to this day, every individual must ask themselves as they seek the truth of our Father. *Who do you say I am?* To verify this question with the correct answer is both life-saving and necessary.

Jesus knew that those who listened to His teachings understood He was a healer and a miracle worker, but they did not necessarily understand His mission. And so, Jesus posed the question to His disciples as He began to prepare them for the truth of His ministry, *Who do you say I am?* Often this question slips past us as relatively unimportant.

Our relationship seems solid and stable, so the need to answer Jesus's questions seems unnecessary. After all, Christ knows our hearts. This, my friend, is why we should ponder this question and make every effort to answer it. Dr. Brian Arnold referred to Jaroslav Pelikan's remark, "If Christ is risen, nothing else matters. And if Christ is not risen—nothing else matters."[2] Who is Christ to you?

Jesus was unexpected to the crowds. They weren't sure whether to accept this picture of humanity versus what they believed the Messiah would be. They called Him John the Baptist, Elijah, or a prophet of old because they couldn't wrap their heads around this man who was the opposite of what they expected. They wanted to believe but feared the consequences of the old law. It seems that humanity still struggles with who Jesus is, ages later. Seek deep into your soul for the answer of who you believe Jesus is. You may be surprised at the revelation you find.

Besides this you know the time, that the hour has come
for you to wake from sleep. For salvation is nearer to
us now than when we first believed.
—Romans 13:11–12

Children fear the words *end times*. Why? They worry because their understanding is limited to what is temporal. To end means to take away, to stop. Remove. A child has difficulty seeing and understanding that eternity is glory forever. Sometimes adults are equally as naive. The thoughts of eternity only relate to sadness. Perhaps the loss of a loved one. The spiritual realm never clicks.

Paul spent a significant amount of time throughout his ministry reminding people there was more than the temporal. There was the eternal as well, so his message was urgent when he wrote to the church in Rome. Wake up! The coming of Christ is close.

Paul's call to the Romans was to become aware, step out of their blatant sin, and prepare for what was to come. Now that Jesus had come and become the sacrifice for our sin, He would return. This time, not as the teacher or sacrifice, but as the Savior, and He would take His people into eternity with Him. Be ready for the eternal.

As humans, we live in the moment. Anything that moves us away from the comforts of what we know becomes something we try to avoid. We have difficulty looking toward eternity because it's beyond what we know and understand. When we move to challenge the depth of our beliefs in Christ, the temporal begins to crumble away, and the joy and great expectation of eternity in glory peer through. Suddenly the power of the Almighty grasps hold, and our longing for the heavenly things becomes a hunger. Live your life toward Christ, and there is nothing to fear. Be ready to be taken into the arms of a loving Savior.

Day 47

Do not be conformed to this world,
but be transformed by the renewal of your mind.
—Romans 12:2

One of our generation's great apologists, R. C. Sproul, said while explaining the state of humanity and the transformation of their souls:

The Bible tells us that we are called as Christian people not to be conformed to this world but be transformed . . . and the way of that transformation is through the renewing of the mind. We have been made by our Creator to have a direct line from the brain, or the mind, to the heart . . . and so for the Scripture the new mind brings with it always a new heart. But you can't bypass the mind in an attempt to have a renewed heart. And that is what people are trying to do today. "I don't want to learn . . . I don't want to study the Word of God. I want to have a feeling . . . some mystical experience. And let that . . . replace the hard studies of the content of the Word of God." But the way the Scriptures say life changes is when the mind changes.[3]

Conforming to the world is easy when it offers us all the tantalizing desires of humanity. Every weakness that lives within us releases to the pleasures provided by a fallen world. We easily believe there is nothing wrong with our lust for worldly desires. After all, we assume God wants us to have *all* the desires of our hearts, prosperity, and wealth when instead, He wants our souls transformed.

Paul understood what transformation meant. He was fully transformed from a murderer of Christians to a faithful servant of Christ. If he was not an example of transformation from the world, nothing is. The day his mindset changed, so did his heart. Understandably, this was a clear and practiced teaching gained from Christ. It was not an easy change. Imagine his hardships from those he'd persecuted. Trust was a vital issue when he began to preach Christ. People had to not only hear of his transformation, but they had to see it. Was this the thorn in the flesh he described? Through his own imprisonment and persecutions, Paul was changed by the body and in his mind. Allow Christ to transform your heart and mind. Life changes when the heart and mind change.

Day 48

Sanctify them in the truth; your word is truth.
—John 17:17

There is more power in these nine words than man can imagine. It's incredible at the depth involved here. To dissect every part of these nine words requires prayer and study. From truth. What is truth? To sanctify, and what does sanctify mean? How do we attain sanctification? Jesus's prayer in John 17 was not for Himself but His disciples, and it was deep, sincere—even pleading.

When Pilate asked Jesus if He was a king, Jesus replied, "For this purpose I was born and for this purpose I have come into the world—to bear witness to the truth." He succinctly annunciated what and who He was—truth. So when we connect these things, we begin to see what He prayed for His disciples. He asked the Father to sanctify, make them holy in Him, set apart, consecrated, and a hallowed people for *Him*. This prayer of protection exemplifies the love Christ had for them. He knew the world would persecute His followers. He understood, better than anyone, what lay ahead for them, but He desired that God sanctify them in truth because His Word "was with God, and the Word was God" (John 1:1) and was holy and sacred. He knew they would have to continue to grow in their relationship with God even after He returned to the Father. The positional sanctification they received upon their acceptance of Jesus would have to become a progressive sanctification, a growing process as they drew closer to Him. By understanding this first and foremost: Christ was the truth and that the truth was God, the growth of the disciples became enriched and strengthened. If we take this further, it is likewise for us.

Sanctified through the *Truth*—Christ Jesus—to the Father by *His Word*, Himself. What a tender yet ultimately powerful prayer.

But I am not ashamed, for I know whom I have believed,
and I am convinced that he is able to guard until that
day what has been entrusted to me.
—2 Timothy 1:12

D aniel W. Whittle penned a chorus in 1883 that became one of the most beautiful testimonies of faith in his time. Captured straight from the Word, this hymn speaks volumes about faith, trust, and the assurance found in Christ.

But "I know whom I have believed,
and am persuaded that He is able
to keep that which I've committed
unto Him against that day."[4]

Paul wrote his letter to Timothy during his second imprisonment. Most likely chained in the depths of a dungeon and exposed to the elements, he was well aware his life was nearing an end. Paul loved and respected Timothy so much that he lovingly referred to him as a beloved son. When he wrote this letter, it was to encourage this young man to remain faithful and to carry on the work after he was gone. As he wrote this letter, he explained the hardships he'd faced, reminding Timothy not to be ashamed of him (Paul) or the Christ they followed. His words became an uplifting anthem for Paul and for those who followed. His complete trust in God shines as he shares his conviction that all he has committed to the Lord will stand against anything that might come. Paul prepared his heart and readied his soul for his final days before entering heaven.

How often are we fully convinced of God's faithfulness and His ability? In our human frailty, we quickly falter, yet God never sways. He is the constant and the promise of humanity. In a world of chaos, believe fully in the loyalty of the Father to His children. He is able. He is willing. And He stands firm and committed throughout our trials.

Week 8—Tell the World What God Has and Has Not Done

Hear out the logic in this thought process. Christians love God. In fact, we love Him so much that we spend time telling others about all the wonderful things He has done. But what if the listener is an unbeliever? What if the person hearing the praises of a God who does wonders doesn't know God? Suddenly the wonders of a good and great God may look sour if they have not experienced Him. "I prayed for my dad to be healed from cancer. He died two days later. God doesn't answer prayers. That's a fairytale, and I won't buy into it."

The one thing we wanted to share about our God has just been flipped against us. One of the saddest remarks is "Christians are liars." We aren't liars, or not in the sense that you think, but in our efforts to share the goodness of God, we fail to fully convey the difficulties—the times God did not answer the prayers the way we wanted. In our efforts to share God's mercies and goodness, we forget to include that sometimes the answer to our prayers is no. Or wait.

The nonbeliever needs to see the whole story. The greatest goodness in the Father is when He says no, it is because He knows what lies ahead. He knows if we wait, things work out in His timing.

When we share our stories of Christ's goodness in our lives, don't forget what it took to get to the other side. Don't let the world take away the hope we find in Christ by allowing the nonbeliever to think our lives are perfect. Let them see the process. Let them hear how your life changed. You may just spark a flame in their heart.

Day 50

And you shall not strip your vineyard bare, neither shall you
gather the fallen grapes of your vineyard. You shall leave them
for the poor and for the sojourner: I am the LORD your God.
—Leviticus 19:10

We seem to have things backward. Continuously the Lord reminds us to care for the poor, but never once does He say take away their dignity. Moses, the presumed writer of Leviticus, took great pains to lay out dos and don'ts for the people. His direction, given to him by God, outlined specifics to help the people maintain a certain dignity of sorts. Work was one of those things.

Just as in the ancient world, some dread work and prefer a handout in today's world. We've lost our dignity when a handout is better than the privilege of work. When Moses guided the landowners not to strip their vineyards bare, His reason was apparent. What was left became the spoils for the poor or the wanderer. It was a way of giving back from their wealth, but it was also a provision, not a handout. The spoils were left for the poor to gather. They were not collected for the poor, and this was important. Though the poor might be dependent on the leftovers, they were able to work to gather the food and this, in essence, allowed them to have a purpose. The spoils were there but collecting them was their responsibility. A man's dignity remained, and the appreciation of both provision and the ability to work allowed purpose for even those unable to perform a trade.

Caring for the poor doesn't mean taking away their dignity found in being self-sustaining. It means making sure there are things available for those in need to collect for themselves. God was allowing the poor the fulfillment of providing for themselves. As we study God's Word and see how He carefully laid out His guidelines, we see the depth of His love. Study His Words. Follow His ways. Love as He loves. Find the dignity He desires for you.

The saying is trustworthy and deserving of full
acceptance, that Christ Jesus came into the world
to save sinners, of whom I am the foremost.
—1 Timothy 1:15

I f ever a verse was chock-full of truth, it's here. Bathed in truth from
the word *trustworthy* to Christ coming to the world to save sinners
and ending with Paul's admission of being a sinner, we cannot deny
what is held here.

Paul opens by using the word *trustworthy*, a clear statement that this is
not only a creed we can rest on, but it is a dependable doctrine. This truth
of Christ has and will continue to stand the test of time. Count on it.

He then leads us to a second truth: Christ came into the world to
save sinners. As Christians, we call that a given, but it's more. When we
stop and ponder the truth that Christ, God incarnate, came into the
world because His love for us was so great. God does not want to lose even
one of His children to darkness, and to prove that He came in the form of
man—something we could understand—and by His blood of humanity,
He suffered and died to save us from sin. It is almost more than we can
absorb when we truly ponder the depth of the sacrifice.

Finally, Paul's admittance of his sin is laid firmly before us. Paul, a man
transformed from nearly unforgivable acts, was made clean, whole, and
purified through the blood of Christ. It is easy to say that Christ came to
save the sinner, but it is more than challenging to admit that the sinners He
came to save are you and me.

This word is trustworthy and true. It is a sound doctrine given entirely
to the sinner who is now saved by the blood. Soak in this text. Take it in,
and then praise the sacrifice given on your behalf.

He brought me out into a broad place; he rescued me,
because he delighted in me.
—Psalm 18:19

Many claim to pray. Claiming and doing are two different things. Some pray beautiful heartfelt prayers at the drop of a hat, while others struggle to find words. Many pray in solitude while others pray short arrow prayers through the day, but those who pray in the cover of darkness, cry out with all their hearts. They pray when no one else stirs. They pace the floor, lifting their hearts in lament to the Father. There is a desperation to their prayers given in darkness, and they pray in the deliverance of God, trusting in the light that will come. Often not knowing what to pray, "the Spirit himself intercedes," as Romans 8:26 states.

The Psalmist, David, wrote and sang psalms fervently. They were his prayer journal of sorts. In his book of joy, fear, pain, peace, and even rest is where he found the presence of God. Psalm 18 is a prayer prayed in the cover of darkness. It was a prayer of gratefulness, thanksgiving, and recognition of all God had done for him. This prayer bellowed from the depths of David's heart because he understood he would have or be nothing without the Father who loved and cared for him fully. David acknowledged that God rescued him and, more so, that God delighted in him, a child of his own through that rescue.

What a beautiful thing, as the world sleeps, when we can fall to our knees and cry out in the night, assured God could split the darkness wide open, exposing our sins. Then with His breath gently blow them away. This type of prayer requires a willing vulnerability, one many are not willing to offer, but when they do—oh, what peace they find. Pray under cover of darkness. Expose your shortcomings, your sin. Become vulnerable and God will fill you to overflowing.

Day 53

The soldiers' plan was to kill the prisoners, lest any should swim away and escape. But the centurion, wishing to save Paul, kept them from carrying out their plan. He ordered those who could swim to jump overboard first and make for the land.

—Acts 27:42–43

Unbelievers accuse the Christian of attempting to convince them the life of a believer is perfect. When we come upon problems, we pray and poof—in some miraculous way, God gleefully answers our prayer just the way we planned it. What a misconception. However, it does partially ring true. We are quick to tell unbelievers of the wonders of God, His provision, and help, but rarely do we stop to say there were hardships along the way. Our Father does love us completely, but through our troubles and trials, He grooms us to be more Christlike. God often offers us miraculous resolution, but it is not truthful to allow others to think the answer came to us without work. This misleads the unbeliever.

Paul certainly maneuvered his share of hardships along the way, but he never said God's answers were easy. And he never stopped sharing the difficulties. After all, Paul was living proof. Yet through Paul's suffering, his faith grew stronger, and the souls he reached, even in prison, were innumerable. God promised to deliver him on this trip to Rome, but Paul was tossed about fourteen days on a stormy sea. Did God deliver? Yes. Was it bells and bows? No. Then what could Paul possibly gain from this trial? Strength in God's promises. Reassurance the Father is faithful. Joy even in jumping overboard to float on broken ship planks until they hit land. Do not be afraid to share your stories of hardship and how God made a way. "It was the soldiers' plan to kill the prisoners." Yet the centurion didn't. Paul shared the hardship. Share those things so that those who do not know Him understand what faith is and that they too might long for what you have in Christ.

Day 54

Do your best to present yourself to God as one approved,
a worker who has no need to be ashamed,
rightly handling the word of truth.
—2 Timothy 2:15

It is not our calling to present ourselves approved before man. Instead, we must show ourselves approved to the Father. Putting our best efforts forward in all we do for Him is what counts. What if our work, even if it is our best, falls short by man's evaluation? The question then becomes, who is man that he should judge what our best efforts are?

Paul, the writer of this letter to Timothy, wanted to make Timothy understand what his work as a minister of the Word would require. It needed to be his best. Not in the eyes of man, but in the eyes of God, whom he would represent. He knew there would be times when Timothy would face difficulty and extreme circumstances. Paul encouraged him not to be ashamed of the work he would do but to stand firm in his handling of the Word, since he had to lovingly, yet firmly, express the mishandling of God's word by men who tried to live by the old law and the new law simultaneously.

Our world thrives on twisting meanings by taking portions of our words out of context and then representing them as truth. Of all times, now is when we must study God's Word and know it, for the world wants God removed from sight so it can do as it pleases without guilt.

Spend time in the Word. Present yourself to God as one approved. Do not fear or be ashamed of the Father or of handling His Word in truth. He will stand by you as you work diligently to teach a lost and dying world.

Day 55

Remember the Sabbath day, to keep it holy. Six days
you shall labor, and do all your work, but the seventh
day is a Sabbath to the LORD your God.
—Exodus 20:8–10

Theologians say God instituted the Sabbath for man, not man
for the Sabbath. Jesus said it. Though it sounds somewhat
contradicting, it isn't. Simply stated, God worked for six days. He
rested on the seventh. We could say, God is mighty. Rest is not necessary
for the Almighty, and though that may be true, God doesn't always
exist for Himself. He is not a selfish God, in the respect that He wants
everything as His own. Instead, the Father loves to care for His children,
and when He worked for six days, He set a precedent for His children.
"I worked for six days, and you can too, but man needs rest. Rest on the
Sabbath. Keep it holy. Remember what I have done for you." He did not
create man for that day—instead, it was the opposite.

Man's efforts to obey God's commands failed miserably. We see
continuously throughout Scripture how man instituted overzealous
restrictions that bound the people so tightly that even walking outside
their homes broke the law.

God has always been clear about His laws, and there is always a solid
reason why He placed guidelines for man to follow. Out of His purest
love and care, He offered rules to maintain order for easily swayed and
overindulgent people. Even today, we overwork. Rest is fleeting as too
much bounty eats away our time. We demand the luxury of much, but we
gain it at the risk of losing our souls. God's laws were not a way to torture
His people. God knew well what we could do to ourselves. His law was to
protect man from himself. Imagine if we followed this law, to rest on the
Sabbath and keep it holy, what it would do to reinstitute the sacred status
of the family. Listen to God. Rest. Keep Him holy.

But I with the voice of thanksgiving will sacrifice to you; what I have
vowed I will pay. Salvation belongs to the Lord!
—Jonah 2:9

No one likes to admit when they are wrong. It goes against our nature. Worse yet—our pride. When it becomes blatantly apparent the choice we've made was a bad one, admission becomes, for lack of better words, crow.

God has gifted us with free will. It had to be difficult because His desire is for us to love Him by choice, not force. Yet even in His desire for us to love Him freely, He as a loving Father still gently guides us. Sometimes, God has plans for us individually, and when this happens, He may push harder for our obedience. Whether we come into compliance does not prevent God's will and plan from moving ahead. His ways are bigger, stronger, and better than ours. When we refuse to obey, when we think we know best, God will allow us to suffer the consequence of a bad choice. It doesn't mean He doesn't love us, but it does prove His ways are far better.

Jonah had no intention of doing what God wanted. His prejudice toward the Ninevites and his idea of what he thought should happen led him to make a bad decision. God let him, but in doing so Jonah reaped the consequence. When he realized his sin and that God rescued him despite his stubbornness, Jonah grew thankful. He admitted he was wrong.

Confessing our sin is the first step of true repentance. Changing our ways is the next. Thankfulness for forgiveness follows. Our Father is a loving God. We can call Him Abba and understand Abba will love and yes, discipline His children. When we obey God's call, wonderful things happen through that obedience. It's not always easy, but it is always right.

Week 9—God's Unfathomable Love for Us

I t is hard to comprehend the love of God. Better yet, to understand why this God of the universe has such love for a fallen group like humanity. Yet, His love is unfailing, unending, and we can go a step further and remember that He delights in us.

Even saying *wow* doesn't effectively cover the immensity of His love for us. Through the ages, God has loved mankind dearly. He did, after all, create us to be fruitful, and through our fruitfulness, we bring Him glory.

Our deeper relationship depends on our continuance of seeking greater knowledge. That knowledge comes by spending time in His Word, doing our best to bring Him glory. There is so much we don't know or can't know about an omniscient God. His ability to skirt through time allows Him to know what was, what is, and what will be. Still, God's love for us remains unfathomable.

He provides for our needs. His faithfulness is unwavering, and His blessings over us are endearing.

For those staunch in their disbelief, the goal has grown to prove God's love is not real, that life without Him is not so bad. They post billboards flaunting they don't need God, and they shout on television that they don't fear the fires of hell. But we, know better, so we cling to faith, trust, and this unfathomable love, given so freely.

As you read this week, take time to recognize those things that make God real to you. Take in His blessings, from the smallest to the greatest. Welcome Him in so that you can experience the fullness of the Father. Let Him be real. Close out the world. Open your arms to the peace found in Him. And then, do all you can to bring Him glory.

With his mouth the godless man would destroy his neighbor,
but by knowledge the righteous are delivered.
—Proverbs 11:9

I t only takes one misspoken word to wound a life, yet do we guard our words? We fail to think through the consequences of what we say. Once spoken, words can never be rescinded, never taken back. Instead, they remain in the hearts and minds of others forever.

Solomon is credited with writing most of the Proverbs. Some are filled with prophetic wisdom, while many read profoundly toward the common person. It doesn't take long for Solomon to address the tongue—our words. While many Scripture versions call the mouth of the godless man a hypocrite, the meaning doesn't change. When the mouth spouts out lies about its neighbors, it comes from a godless person with little or no regard for the hearts of others. It wounds and ruins those who hear the lies by leading them astray, and it breaks the heart of God.

Even in today's world, the absolutes of God are twisted, torn away, and turned so that those spewing hypocrisy never consider the consequences of their words. Innocent men are imprisoned or murdered because of lies that mislead others down the wrong path. Solomon understood this. He experienced it himself as King. Words can kill, but truth sustains. Its knowledge saves. Jesus came so that we might know the truth, know Him, and know the Father. He spoke words that delivered and changed the hearts of men for the better. Think about your words, whether expressed in constructive criticism or praise. Be honest and trustworthy but be kind even as you offer a rebuke. Remember your words always make a difference.

Day 58

No unbelief made him waver concerning the promise of God,
but he grew strong in his faith as he gave glory to God, fully
convinced that God was able to do what he had promised.
—Romans 4:20–21

Few can say they never waver in their faith or trust in God. We are human. Our sinful nature quickly convinces us that we know what is best. Our faith wanes, and we think at the moment we can fix any issue, any hardship—or at least give it our best effort. Why wait on God? It never fails that our ways are weak and unsustainable.

God promised Abraham he would be the father of nations, and Abraham never stopped believing that God would keep His promise, even when he had no idea how or when God would follow through. His faith brought him to be called righteous. Even when Abraham and Sarah tried to take things into their own hands and rush the promise along, Abraham did not stop believing in God's promise.

How fortunate are we that God understands our human impulses and forgives our efforts to take matters into our own hands? He doesn't prevent the consequence, but He forgives our choices. Of course, we should make every effort to trust fully in God, but our staunch belief in His promises and in Him brings us the title of righteous. If we would only remain faithful, what amazing things God could and would do through us.

Mary Kay Ashe, the founder of Mary Kay Cosmetics, once said, "Much is lost but for one last effort." There is great truth in this thought when we apply it to our spiritual lives. We will gain so much more if we simply make that one last push to believe God in His promises. He is faithful. Look deep into your heart and learn to believe. God will keep His promises.

Day 59

I have said these things to you, that in me you may
have peace. In the world you will have tribulation.
But take heart; I have overcome the world.
—John 16:33

I have overcome. Sometimes simply seeing the words of Jesus drives home the most profound meaning. Do we always understand? No, but when we have it laid out for us to study when we can apply it, suddenly the flood gates open.

Often the disciples, try as they might, simply did not understand what Jesus was saying. It wasn't that they were stupid or dumb, for lack of better words, but they were relearning a new type of law, veering drastically from the law they'd always followed. The things Jesus spoke of were challenging to separate from a literal understanding into a spiritual one. Jesus was oh so patient with His disciples. He understood this. When His time neared an end, Jesus urgently tried to provide insight and comfort for His disciples. The events that would soon fall into play would test the disciples and cause them to fear and question. Jesus took time to reassure them that though He would leave them, He would return. Christ reminded them not to be afraid, that the world would not always be kind. It would test and doubt, even attack them, but He overcame! That changed it all. What encouragement and reassurance. He will return: a promise made, a promise kept upon His resurrection, and a promise that will be honored upon His second coming. When frustrations and difficulties test and try you, remember the promise of Jesus. Remember His command. Take heart! He has overcome. The best is yet to come.

Day 60

Then he said to me, "This is the word of the
LORD to Zerubbabel: Not by might, nor by power,
but by my Spirit, says the LORD of hosts."
—Zechariah 4:6

This day and time, we face extreme pressure and circumstances in living out our spiritual beliefs. The world fights relentlessly to oppress and even annihilate our efforts. Just as they were persecuted in the time of Jesus, believers are still persecuted today. Even in our nation, built as one under God, evil forces work to take away the absolutes of our beliefs in Christ.

Cyrus released the Jewish exiles and sent them under the care of Zerubbabel, along with the High Priest Joshua, to rebuild the Temple. It was not an easy task, and roadblocks came that seemed impossible to overcome. But God charged Zerubbabel to begin the rebuild, though Zerubbabel and Joshua were unsure how this would happen. God reminded them: it wouldn't be done by might or power, but it would be successful because of My Spirit. The Spirit of God would intervene and overcome the obstacles that man tried to place underfoot.

Herein lies the critical gem in this scripture. The Spirit of God is mighty, and the Father's plans cannot be thwarted by anything. What He has moved to achieve within His plan will come about in God's timing. Not by power or might, but by the will of God Almighty.

The same is true within the confines of our earthly lives. God's plan for us may not be seen clearly or even understood as to how, why, or when, but God knows. Just because we are not privy to the details does not mean He will not accomplish the task. Ours is the job to trust and believe that God will do what He says He will do. Don't worry when you don't understand the "how comes." Simply look up and trust that the Lord, through His Spirit, will accomplish the tasks He has set in motion in your life.

Day 61

The LORD bless you and keep you; the LORD make his face to shine upon you and be gracious to you; the LORD lift up his countenance upon you and give you peace. So shall they put my name upon the people of Israel, and I will bless them.
—Numbers 6:24–27

The word *Nazirite* comes from the Hebrew word *nazar*, which means "to separate or dedicate oneself to." They were unique individuals, not necessarily chosen but who volunteered for this office, taking an equally special vow. They gave their service and their hearts entirely to God, and in this giving, accepted the Nazirite laws of obedience: to abstain from drinking intoxicants, cutting his/her hair, and touching a corpse. Though their jobs were not exactly clear, their desire to serve God entirely was.

Previously, the Nazirite law is given, the dos and don'ts for those who have offered themselves to God, so when Aaron offered this prayer and blessing at this particular time, it was a bit surprising. God spoke to Moses and told him to have Aaron and his sons speak to the people, not just the Nazirites but the people of Israel and offer this blessing. It was a blessing God specifically worded, which made it even more meaningful and powerful.

"The Lord bless you and keep you." Those whom God blesses are indeed loved and blessed. "The Lord make his face to shine upon you." God shines over those He cherishes as the sun rises and brings renewal. His goodness is beyond all we can imagine. "The Lord lift up his countenance upon you." The expressions of God—just as a father smiles over his children, He shows pleasure, joy, and peace. "So shall they put my name upon the people of Israel, and I will bless them." This was an ahh moment when God lovingly stamped His name on His people of choice and His love. You are chosen, loved, and blessed. What more could you desire? May He shine over you.

Day 62

"If you would be perfect, go, sell what you possess and
give to the poor, and you will have treasure in heaven;
and come, follow me." . . . The young man . . . went
away sorrowful. . . . "It is easier for a camel to go
through the eye of a needle than for a rich
person to enter the kingdom of God."
—Matthew 19:21–22, 24

Throughout the ages, possessions have deemed our status. The more you own, the wealthier you are, but where does that put us when we look at our spiritual wealth? Jesus poses the thought that anyone with riches could not enter heaven, so does that mean no wealthy individuals will be in heaven? Though Jesus goes on to say, "all things are possible with God," the idea here is whether money has its grip on you, or do you have a hold on money? Who rules whom?

Scripture gives us little information on this young man. Was he indeed a ruler, did he hold an office, or was he simply a fortunate individual, blessed with financial wealth? Either way, the point Jesus makes doesn't change when he stated it was easier for a camel to pass through the eye of the needle than for a rich person to enter heaven. Be this a literal analogy or symbolic, this young man was not willing. He walked away from Jesus, sad because he had great wealth. He prided himself on walking in the law, yet his gloating only proved his piousness and greed. He couldn't let go of the temporal to gain the eternal.

Whatever your wealth: financial, success, or work, it comes down to letting go. Are you willing to release it and follow Jesus fully? God knows our lack of perfection, and His sacrifice freed us entirely. He unloaded our burden so we could pass through the eye. Loosen your white-knuckle grip and follow Christ fully.

Day 63

And the LORD said to Samuel, "Obey the voice of the people
in all that they say to you, for they have not rejected you,
but they have rejected me from being king over them."
—1 Samuel 8:7

Sometimes our ways are harsh. In our ability to think we have all the answers, man will hurt those they love the most. Our sinful natures assume we are more significant, more robust, and wiser than the God who created us. When our attitudes grow cocky, we hurt others. That includes breaking the heart of God.

We can never assume to know what God is thinking or feeling, but by the very tone of this conversation, it is evident that the heart of God breaks.

Samuel took this cry as a personal attack against his leadership when the people insisted on a king, someone to lead them and fight their battles. God quickly reassured him that it was not about him. "They have rejected me from being king over them." In essence, the people broke their covenant relationship with God, and therein, laid their sin.

Throughout the years, God had remained faithful to His children. He provided, cared for, and protected them over and over. Imagine the slap in the face He must have felt to have His children raise a palm toward Him so that they could be like others. Their relationship with God set them apart from all else. How could they be so blind as to ignore that?

As believers, we are quick to tell others we serve God, but we decline His leadership and plans for us equally as fast. The question then becomes how deeply do we believe in the Father who created us and in His continued care and promises?

The heart of God must have ached when He told Samuel to give them a king. Yet still, God faithfully loved His children. Search your heart. What do you believe?

Week 10—He Knows Your Name

God knows your name. Isn't that profound? Think about it. The God of all creation, the Almighty, powerful, and eternal God, knows your name. Better yet, He knew you before you were born. This loving God cared so much about you that He meticulously chose your hair color, size, and abilities, and He wrote them in His heart. In all His glory, He knows your every thought and feeling, and not only does He know you, but He knows us all equally the same.

How can God know every intimate detail about us, much less hear every individual prayer? But this is the magnificent God we call Abba.

In a world of doubters, this is one element that is thrown back in the face of the Christian. The dilemma becomes how to explain what is unexplainable. How can we describe an omnipotent God? We can't. At least not in words. Who God is shows in our lives. Oh, we can easily say He is mighty. He is everywhere. He is the creator of all things, but that is only scratching the surface of the Father who knows who you are.

This Father is so involved in you, so invested, that He said, "[insert your name], I sent my Son to die for you."

Reincorporating a revived Christian worldview into our lives requires work. It requires our belief and prayer. More so, it requires the *world* seeing Christ in and through you.

He knows your name, but do you really know His? I Am, Abba Father, Adonai, Lord, Emmanuel, God with Us. Do you know His Name?

Spend time this week comprehending that He knows your name, and then get to know His so that through you, others will see.

Day 64

For this light momentary affliction is preparing for us an
eternal weight of glory beyond all comparison, as we look
not to the things that are seen but to the things that are unseen.
For the things that are seen are transient, but the things
that are unseen are eternal.
—2 Corinthians 4:17–18

"God, show me a sign! Help me! Where are you?" Who hasn't fallen to their knees before and cried out like this to God? There are times our burdens, the things we suffer, drive us to the point of no return, and we cry out, "Abba Father." And then . . . we hear crickets. No answer. No sound. The God who offers us the promise of always being there—isn't. Or we think He isn't.

We know God never leaves us, nor is He a Father who makes empty promises, yet we are impatient people. We insist on instant gratification. Our lives center around what is *now*, not what is to come. Perhaps our human frailty drives us to look only into the next moment. Eternity is the furthest thing from our minds.

Paul offered encouragement to the people. He implied his suffering and his peers' suffering in the Christ they believed was nothing compared to what was to come. Eternity. Faith is a unique thing. It takes us from what we can hold in our hands to only what we believe. Our sufferings or losses here on earth are transient, here one moment and gone the next, but that which we cannot see, our faith in God, stretches out to e-t-e-r-n-i-t-y. Forever. Paul did his best to help the people understand that what happens here and now is only a moment, but forever with God withstands all else. The sacrifice is worth it. Look into your heart. Decide where your focus should be, the here and now or the hope of eternity. Now look toward that goal.

Day 65

In the beginning was the Word, and the Word was
with God, and the Word was God. He was in the beginning
with God. All things were made through him, and without
him was not any thing made that was made. In him was life,
and the life was the light of men.
—John 1:1–4

I magine being John, the one Jesus loved, the one who walked in the
inner circle of Christ. Imagine standing in awe at this gentle man
called Jesus, listening as He reads from scripture, as He tenderly
makes the Word come alive and then suddenly realizing that He, Himself,
is the Word. He was, is, and always will be. Try to take in this revelation.

Though Scripture holds many unique and profound thoughts, these
verses pull together the deity and person of Christ. There are times that
the person Jesus seems so far away from us. We cannot stretch out our
hands and touch Him as John and the other disciples could. Even in
their physical presence of Christ, they struggled to wrap their minds
around God as a man, Abba Father in human form. The God of the
Law now stood before them in a form they could fathom. This God they
worshipped was so much more than the law they knew. He was firm, but
He was gentle, tender, loving, and He desired a relationship with them.

Still, when John opens his writing with the finite description of
Christ, we can feel the sudden realization he must have felt. Before Him
indeed was God Almighty. We can only guess at the fullness the disciples
saw and felt as they walked the dirt roads with Christ, but this scripture
not only opens our eyes to the reality of Christ, it sums Him up beautifully.
The deity and the man come together, so we might understand—that we
might be saved. This Christ, a different side of God the Father, brought
about a new understanding of who He is. One of love and compassion,
not strictly law. This effort to make humanity see the depths of His love
still amazes.

Day 66

God said to Moses, "I AM WHO I AM." And he said, "Say this to the
people of Israel: 'I AM has sent me to you.'"
—Exodus 3:14

"I AM WHO I AM." Mighty words from a powerful God. His own description of Himself speaks to His omniscience. It shouts out His omnipotence and His omnipresence. Nothing about God is fleeting. He has been, shall be, and is ever present. When He spoke His name to Moses, God was giving Moses His personal name. Without a doubt, it was the name Israel knew that set Him apart from all else. The Great I AM.

There are moments when the timeline of our lives interferes with our understanding of God. We do our best to place Him inside our time frame when God knows no boundaries in time. He is present now and was present in the past, so when He calls Himself I AM, He solidifies Himself as the mighty and powerful One—as God.

John mentions seven other times where Jesus states His position as the Son of God. Jesus said, "I am the bread of life," "I am the light of the world," "I am the door of the sheep," "I am the good Shepherd," "I am the resurrection and the life," "I am the way, the truth, and the life," and "I am the true vine." Each time He gently shows His authority, His place in the nature and trinity of God. We could even say this when the soldiers came for Jesus in the garden. He asked them, "Whom do you seek?" Their response was, "Jesus of Nazareth." Jesus then stated, "I am he." (18:4–6) They pulled back and fell to the ground at that sign of authority. I AM, two small words that carried tremendous power.

There is but one I AM. Seek Him and only Him, for He is the Great I AM.

Day 67

I am the good shepherd. I know my own and my own
know me, just as the Father knows me and I know the
Father; and I lay down my life for the sheep.
—John 10:14–15

Name tags are vital for conference faculty, especially if they see returning conferees yearly. Faces are familiar, but the names become blurred after a bit of time. Seeing a name tag saves the embarrassment of a slipping memory, but what if you didn't need a name tag? What if you already knew every person who approached you, even though you'd never met them face-to- face?

This is Jesus—was Jesus. Imagine sitting at His feet as He took the time to express how deeply He loves you. Imagine His looking you in the eye and very pointedly saying, "I lay down my life for the sheep." You would suddenly understand the depth of love this man, this *Son of Man*, has for you.

Jesus longed for those He taught to understand the intimate knowledge God the Father, Christ Himself, had for them. When He likens Himself to the good shepherd, it is easy for the people to understand the relationship. Jesus took them one step deeper to remind them that just as a shepherd guards his flock literally with his life (there were insurmountable dangers in the fields at night from predators, robbers, and more), He too would lay down His life for the sheep. This was a foreshadowing of what was to come.

To be known fully by the Father is more than special, and understanding His deep involvement in us is even greater. We are not leaves blowing aimlessly in the wind, but we are fully known, to the deepest core of our beings, fully loved and sacrificed for wholly. Each one of us is important, and He knows us all. No name tag is necessary. Our names are written on His heart.

I am the vine; you are the branches. Whoever abides in
me and I in him, he it is that bears much fruit, for
apart from me you can do nothing.
—John 15:5

A nalogies help us understand. They draw pictures in our minds.
Help us relate. Draw interest. Without them, our conversation
and our learning would be flat. The human mind absorbs
stories, and teachers understand that, especially when teaching young
children. The comparison found in the analogies of small stories helps
us comprehend.

Jesus knew this. He knew many of the people He taught would have
little or no education, so He brought things down to a level that made
sense—simple, everyday life stories and analogies.

In using the analogy of the vine and branches, Jesus was able to
communicate fully not only His position in the headship but the rewards
of a relationship with that headship. This image of the branches drawing
the necessary life-giving things helped Jesus convey that living and
drawing, depending on Him alone, was spiritually the best place to reside.
The thought He offered the people to *abide in Him* was a heartfelt gift.
He desired to share with those who not only walked with Him daily but
with those He taught along the way.

The person, the Christ, loved people. All people. God, Christ
incarnate, loved and still loves us unconditionally. We are nothing without
Him because all things are made through Him and in Him. Jesus, though
ultimately God the Father, lived His life in accordance with the Father. He
drew His strength from God. When Jesus separated Himself away from the
group to pray, He was doing exactly what He offered us in this scripture, to
abide with the Father. Draw from Him. Find the end of yourself. Be who
He calls you to be and stay in the One who offers spiritual happiness.

For thus said the Lord GOD, the Holy One of Israel, "In returning and rest you shall be saved; in quietness and in trust shall be your strength."
—Isaiah 30:15

There's an Appalachian phrase that bears not only humor but significant truth: "running around like a chicken with its head cut off." The people of the deep Appalachian culture weren't always book smart, but they were undoubtedly *life* smart. The truth behind this phrase speaks for itself.

God often used Isaiah to warn the people of the consequences of their evil ways, even when the words fell on deaf ears. At this moment in time, the people were "running around like a chicken with its head cut off." They faced the rise of Assyria, and their first thought was to run directly to Egypt for protection. Isaiah was doing his best to convince them their choices were not wise. He preached their strength was not in themselves or even in Egypt. Their salvation lay with God and only God. It was time to stop trying to fix things themselves. Return to God. Rest in Him and be saved.

Many times, we are as blind as the children of Israel. In our determination to fix situations immediately, we move from God and stand in His way. Impatience and stubbornness guide our reactions rather than sitting quietly in Him and allowing God to do what He has promised. Our efforts often stamp that Appalachian phrase straight on our foreheads. Isaiah tried to convey this message then, but he still conveys it through the Word. Stop "running around like a chicken with your head cut off" and sit still. Pray. Listen. Trust. God is faithful—always.

•

Day 70

So to keep me from becoming conceited because of the
surpassing greatness of the revelations, a thorn was given
me in the flesh, a messenger of Satan to harass me,
to keep me from becoming conceited.
—2 Corinthians 12:7

There's nothing worse than pain. Continual discomfort makes us miserable. Statistics are said to show that Americans alone spend $17.8 billion per year on prescription medications to improve their pain but imagine being Paul.

When Paul mentions he was given a thorn in the flesh, two things jump out. First, he said explicitly, "a messenger of Satan to harass me," so it was prominent and noticeable. Secondly, perhaps it was a reminder or a stern warning for him to hold a once conceited and determined attitude humble and authentic to the Spirit.

Often, we assume much into this verse. We cannot answer questions like did God assign this thorn, or did Satan use this as an attack? Was it relational? Given his past, consider the frustrations and hardships Paul had to overcome as he taught the very people he persecuted. Indeed, a thorn such as this would plague his ministry. Imagine trying to enter a town he'd persecuted and rebuild trust. Though scripture doesn't make us privy to his reference here, we know whatever followed him, be it spiritual, physical, or relational, was something to contend with. "Count it all joy" was the attitude Paul maintained. Rather than falling to the thorn, he looked directly to the one who freed him and worked to keep him on track.

The question becomes, how do you manage pain? Rarely do we consider it pure joy, but our pain could certainly groom us to be better. Whatever Paul's affliction was, God continued to use it and Paul to reshape a distorted world. Allowing God to use us through our pain is hard, but we grow exponentially when we do.

Week 11—Where Our Heart Lies

I t's easy to get caught up in our Christianity and forget about our hearts. Our focus falls on ourselves and everything we want, need, or desire. When troublesome times fall over us, our hearts cry out in agony, fully expecting God to grab us up, stroke our backs, and immediately fix the problem. Our discomfort or sadness lies in the forefront, not what God may have in store for our lives.

Sometimes our lives are touched with constant affliction, such as Paul's thorn in the flesh, or it may be a temporary situation that plagues us for a time. It leaves us clueless about how to respond, so we cry out to God for wisdom and discernment.

Jesus spent a lot of time in prayer. Even in His perfection, He called upon the Father for guidance. He even pleaded with God, but everything Jesus did was in accordance with His nature, the nature of God. He did all He could to teach His disciples that when they failed to care for those in need, they failed to care for Him. When He spoke to the young ruler, He told him to sell his possessions and follow Him, but the young man, a bit pious and greedy, was not the man he thought himself to be.

We are not always right in our choices or methods to make a choice. Often, we fail miserably, but God knows our hearts. He knows when we ignore the touch of the Holy Spirit, and He sees through the walls we try to build around our hearts. Lay up your treasures in heaven. Do for your brother as you would do for yourself. Love your neighbor. All these things point to the ultimate question. Do we glorify God through our actions?

As you work through the reading this week, keep that question at the edge of your mind. Examine your heart. Look at your actions. Work to glorify God in everything you do.

Day 71

Then he will answer them, saying, "Truly, I say to you,
as you did not do it to one of the least of these,
you did not do it to me."
—Matthew 25:45

It was said, "If you want to kick Jesus in the gut, ignore the poor. Judge the lowly. Refuse provision and love to the needy." It's a good example that nails how we are quick to judge those we view as imperfect or poor.

Jesus finishes His teaching in this section with a bit of rebuke. He's stern and direct. "As you did not do it to one of the least of these, you did not do it to me." Notice Jesus says, "as you DID NOT do . . . you DID NOT DO it to me." Does that change the meaning? If you do it to them, we tend to say you have done it to me. The answer is debatable that there is no difference, but it seems here the context Jesus is talking about ties into our final judgment. We've had a lifetime to do what He asked, yet we failed. A time will come when it is too late. The opportunity to backtrack is gone. Jesus reminds the people if you didn't do it then, not only did you refuse even the least of man, you also refused Me.

As humans, we live in the present and dwell in the past, but rarely is the future considered. When Christ comes again, there will be a separation, and those who have refused are lost. The Father is in every part of His creation. He offered Himself on the cross because He didn't want to lose even one soul. Still, humanity ignores Him. Still, man does for himself and forgets the simple. Jesus knew what lay ahead for Him. He knew what He would face and the cruelty of it. Jesus walked among those in need despite that knowledge. He cared for every person, regardless of status. Look into your heart and ask, what did I *not do*? Then rectify it before you cannot.

Day 72

Jesus said, "For judgment I came into this world, that those who do not see may see, and those who see may become blind."
—John 9:39

"Though I was blind, now I see." Such poignant words. Words we've seen more than once in the New Testament, words we hear in old hymns, and words carrying an immense meaning. Imagine being blind from birth and never knowing the blue of the sky or green of the trees. Imagine total darkness, no shadows, no light. Blindness impedes, and yet in this scripture, Jesus renders it powerless while at the same time maintaining its grip on some. Confusing? Perhaps a little, but then Jesus was never one to lay out an answer without adding food for thought or an example for better understanding.

Jesus healed the man blind from birth, yet many who'd seen him all his life refused to say this man was truly blind. Even his parents, in fear, said to let him speak for himself when the Pharisees asked. Eventually, they tossed him out, refusing to believe him. Yet Jesus returned to him, already knowing what had transpired, and asked, "Do you believe?" A resounding yes came from the healed man as Jesus introduced Himself as the Son of Man. His affirmation that although the man was physically blind he was also spiritually blind ended when his belief opened his spiritual eyes. Those who thought they knew everything about the law remained in spiritual darkness, blinded and not knowing the beauty found in spiritual sight.

We often proclaim to believe, yet we remain in spiritual blindness, never seeing the truth of Christ Jesus, never going further in our faith than saying, "I believe." The words *I believe* open our spiritual eyes, but the healing begins by stepping into the belief, putting it into action, and allowing it to fill us. Do you genuinely believe? If so, your faith will heal the spiritual blindness, and you will see the Light of the Son of Man.

"Father, glorify your name." Then a voice came from heaven:
"I have glorified it, and I will glorify it again."
—John 12:28

God spoke. This was the second time in the New Testament such a moment occurred. The first was at Jesus's baptism when God audibly spoke. "This is my beloved Son, with whom I am well pleased." (Matthew 3:17). Then here before His arrest and trial and finally, at the transfiguration (Matthew 17:5), "This is my beloved Son . . . listen to him."

The weight of the world was befalling Christ. Now more than ever, there were things He needed to say, complete, and teach before His time on earth ended. Imagine the urgency Christ felt. Since He was human at this point, we can assume there were times the work felt fruitless, His words falling on deaf ears. Yet at this moment, God's voice affirmed Jesus to the crowd, and at the same time, offered a calming reassurance to Jesus, "I am well pleased." Every child needs reassurance at times. Knowing what lay ahead, perhaps those words were for Jesus.

Jesus spent a good amount of time alone in prayer with His Father. We can only imagine the conversations between them, but even knowing His own presence as part of the Godhead Trinity, Christ was obedient to the Father. He loved Him and needed Him. Throughout Jesus's entire ministry, everything He did was purely for the glory of God.

In our daily spiritual walk, we are easily distracted. Our mission can take an about-face, and the focus falls on us rather than God. As we serve, humanity's temptations can slip through. We may not audibly hear God affirm His position, but nonetheless, all glory is His. Christ was the perfect example. Strive to focus all the glory on God. His is the praise. His alone is the glory.

No temptation has overtaken you that is not common to man.
God is faithful, and he will not let you be tempted beyond
your ability, but with the temptation he will also provide
the way of escape, that you may be able to endure it.
—1 Corinthians 10:13

When things are misquoted, we miss out on so much. We often hear this verse quoted: "God will not let you be tempted more than you can withstand." Though this is a truth, there is so much more in the correct wording, for example, the word *ability*. God knows our ability. He knows our breaking point and what will shove us past that.

The context that Paul addressed the Corinthian church about was idolatry. We know idolatry and other immorality are sinful and lead to punishment (Israel is the example, vv. 1–11). Before we think we're better than Old Testament Israel, be careful. This arrogance can lead to our fall. At the same time, take courage because whatever temptations come our way, we can trust that God is faithful and will enable us to endure.

That said, a key phrase is the promise that God "will also provide the way of escape" so that you might endure. In other words, we cannot run from the ethical issues we face. More times than not, the escape is provided through the endurance of the trial and simply through Him. God is faithful, and His promise is true. He will not let you be tempted beyond your ability to endure. Is it easy to wade through challenging scenarios? Certainly not, but when we stand in trust and believe our given promises, God sustains us and equally strengthens us.

Spend time studying the Word. Memorize it and read it in its context. There is depth in the promises of God. Seek out those things and share them accordingly.

Day 75

Count it all joy, my brothers, when you meet trials of various
kinds, for you know that the testing of your faith produces
steadfastness. And let steadfastness have its full effect,
that you may be perfect and complete, lacking in nothing.
—James 1:2–4

Who in their right mind welcomes hardship? The logical consensus is that we make tracks in the opposite direction of trials. Throughout scripture, we're told to be thankful in all things. Paul said, "Rejoice." Still, none of us are raising our hands wishing for difficulty in life, despite the personal growth it might cultivate.

To say the followers and teachers of Christ had a simple and easy life would be far from truthful. Yet, the determination to move forward through the difficulties not only proved their devotion and belief in Christ but made them stronger believers.

When James addressed this issue, he offered encouragement. Perhaps the hardships he addressed were persecution. This was a certainty of the time, but others might have been frustrations of competition, illness, and relationships. Anywhere man can find conflict, he will discover testing.

James takes the automatic negative response of most and challenges them to turn the hardships or testing into a spiritual win. Use those tests to be bigger, stronger, better Christians. "Count it all joy . . . " he says, "when you meet trials." Indeed, it is not an easy thing to do but well worth the effort when we see the good it produces in us. James reminds people that when they build this strength and steadfastness, they will grow toward being perfected and complete in Christ, and in Christ, they lack nothing. It is quite the payoff for patience and endurance in hardship. When you face trials and testing, stand firm. Rejoice. Count it joy for the reward in Christ is worth the effort.

Day 76

> I will remember my covenant that is between me and
> you and every living creature of all flesh. And the waters
> shall never again become a flood to destroy all flesh.
> —Genesis 9:15

In the face of great disaster, it is not uncommon to hear the world rumble that this is God raining down judgment. Man is quick to assume God's intentions. After hurricane Katrina and the devastation it wreaked over New Orleans, the world was fast to think God was showing vengeance over a city they judged as corrupt and sinful.

Fortunately, we are not privy to God's intentions, but we can look at the events of the great flood and draw a conclusion based on God's own words. After the flood, God did not forget Noah, his family, or all the animals He'd protected. Instead, as the waters that covered the entire world receded and life was restored, the Father embraced the faithfulness of Noah. He promised that the waters would never again become a flood to destroy ALL flesh. The operative word is *all*. God made a promise, a covenant, that stands true even today. He did not promise we would never see storms or other devastations, but He promised He'd never destroy all flesh again. When the floodwaters receded, God's promise, a rainbow, was placed in the cloud. To this day just before a downpour or after, that rainbow appears. When the rainbow comes, man does not fail to stop and gaze upon it. Do they all remember the promise? Unfortunately, no, but as believers we do, and our hearts fill with joy. Our job is to help remind the world of a faithful God who keeps His promises. He ended an age of wickedness and began anew. We, too, can start anew by giving our hearts to Him. Will the world see continued threats? Yes. But God's promise is with us, and He will never leave our side. A promise made—a promise still kept.

And the LORD answered me: "Write the vision; make it plain
on tablets, so he may run who reads it. For still the vision awaits its
appointed time; it hastens to the end—it will not lie.
If it seems slow, wait for it; it will surely come; it will not delay."
—Habakkuk 2:2–3

What it must have been like to stand as a prophet of God! Imagine having one-on-one, direct contact with God, receiving direction from Him. Though the book of Habakkuk is small, it packs a punch. Habakkuk's response from God might seem desolate and hopeless, but it's not. It's all in how we broach it. Behind the things to come, lies the promise.

Habakkuk complains, but he makes known that though things look bleak, he will stand and wait. God told him to write the vision he saw— make it plain so people can understand. What a call this was to be placed on Habakkuk when only a few of God's children still held to their beliefs.

Many lean on this verse as the importance of writing things down. There is merit in that. A vision or a dream written down serves as a goal or a reminder, something to help us remember an incident and remember it correctly.

We aren't sure if writing this vision from God was so that a person could literally run with tablets to spread the word or if it refers to the same thing Paul touches on in Hebrews (run the race to completion). Either way, the two things that stand out in importance in this scripture where God gave Habakkuk a vision. First, there is hope for what God would do for His children even with the hardships to come. They needed to see this and to understand it. Secondly, the wait. No one likes to wait, but Habakkuk is reminded, "It will surely come." God often has us stay and wait. We grow, learn, and anticipate what will come in that wait. God's timing is perfect. Write down your thoughts and prayers, hopes and dreams. Write them clearly so you remember, and then patiently wait. "It will surely come; it will not delay."

Week 12—He Listens

The deer at the edge of the forest stand quietly, relaxed. Their heads are bowed, grazing. If you watch, you'll see them gently paw at the earth, foraging for nuts hidden under the leaves, but make one move, one sigh, and their heads rise, ears twitch, and their noses reach upward. Deer hear everything, even hundreds of feet away. They may appear relaxed, but they are always listening, ready to bolt if the warning grows strong.

What kind of listener are you? A mother's senses are amazing. Even with her newborn infant asleep in the next room, she will bolt from a dead sleep if she senses a change in its breathing.

Honing our physical senses takes practice, but what about our spiritual senses? When the Holy Spirit nudges, it's easy to ignore. There may be a nudge to give a little money to the poor man holding a sign by the interstate. Impossible. He should just get a job. Perhaps you have just missed a call from God to act.

Sometimes God's call on our lives is obvious. Maybe we knew from a young age that we felt a special connection to the Father. Perhaps that led to a decision to enter the ministry. Maybe you were so moved by that man on the side of the road that you acted by providing him a meal or starting a nonprofit to aid the homeless. The point is are you listening?

We are called early on to go into the world and teach, make disciples. Jesus repeatedly *called* individuals into service. Our job is to listen and be obedient.

God sees our hearts. In a world that thrives on "what is in it for me," God still calls us to serve. It may be through your church or outside your home. It might be in a card ministry or as a health care worker. Your vocation, passion, and hobby can be a call to service. It's up to us to listen and act.

As you study this week, listen. Ask God to be clear in His nudges, and when you feel them, willingly step up. Your answer to the call may be the one thing that changes a life. Listen and act.

Day 78

But the LORD said to Samuel, "Do not look on his appearance
or on the height of his stature, because I have rejected him.
For the LORD sees not as man sees: man looks on the outward
appearance, but the LORD looks on the heart."
—1 Samuel 16:7

Often, we set unfounded expectations. We quickly look over in-dividuals, even ourselves, assessing things according to our stan-dards. There are times those assessments are necessary, but for the most part, we are not using them in a discerning way. Instead, we lay judgment.

Samuel, despite his position, found himself in this place. He was disappointed in Saul as a king, and he mourned that. And God called Samuel out for it. After all, he'd anointed Saul and placed a blessing over him. Saul failed miserably and God rejected him. When God told Samuel to go to Jesse's household to anoint the next king, immense anxiety covered Samuel. Would Saul kill him? What would others think? Perhaps there was a hint of worry over finding the right person since he mourned Saul's actions. God provided the dialogue for Samuel and guided him to Jesse's home. Samuel's expectations rose as Eliab, Jesse's strapping son, entered, but God quickly thwarted Samuel's expectations. He reminded Samuel, "The Lord looks on the heart."

We can't fool God. His expectations of us are undeniable. Man is good at disguising his attitudes and opinions for others, but God sees through that. There is nothing we can think or do that God isn't blatantly aware. Like a sinful Adam, we try to hide from an omniscient Father. It is hard to admit our fallacies. Dropping that façade before the Father who already knows means acknowledging our sin. God knows our hearts, intentions, and thoughts. He looks at our true nature, and it is here where He judges. Drop your judgmental expectations of yourself and others, for God sees the truth of man in his heart.

Day 79

And if it is evil in your eyes to serve the LORD, choose
this day whom you will serve, whether the gods your
fathers served in the region beyond the River, or the gods
of the Amorites in whose land you dwell. But as for me
and my house, we will serve the LORD.
—Joshua 24:15

Choices are hard, especially when we know what we should choose, but our flesh doesn't agree. Joshua laid down the ultimatum as he prepared to leave. It was time to make the people step up spiritually.

As he spoke to the people, he reminded them of their history. He took them from the exodus, through the wanderings in the wilderness, and into this conquest of Canaan. Joshua didn't hesitate to remind them of their blessings and God's faithfulness, even when they wandered or complained. God multiplied them and brought them to this land of plenty—a land *not* of their labor, nor of cities built by their hands, or of the provision from their efforts. It was all a gift, a fulfillment of His promise.

Joshua publicly committed his love and loyalty to God. By this commitment and the reminder of their history, he showed that the choice should be clear. Their loyalty needed to be toward God, and he offered his and his family's loyalty then and there to God.

We are a lot like the Israelites. Our loyalty and devotion to God waivers with our circumstances. You might think this harsh but recognizing the truth of our sin is never easy. Our ability to compartmentalize our devotion according to our needs is a force to be reckoned with. It is important to remember that God's love and faithfulness never flounders. He is faithful even when we stumble. Examine your faith. Ask yourself, where does my loyalty lie? Is this choice more than a scripture that hangs on a plaque in our home? Count your blessings and recount the number of times God has remained true to you. Then make a choice.

Day 80

Brothers, if anyone is caught in any transgression,
you who are spiritual should restore him in a spirit of
gentleness. Keep watch on yourself, lest you too be tempted.
—Galatians 6:1

Appalachian adages will bring a smile to your day, and though they make you chuckle, there is usually solid reasoning behind them. For example, "I'd like to pinch his head off." Cruel as that sounds, it's not literal. Instead, it's an endearing way of saying I need to correct his behavior.

As Paul finishes speaking of how we walk by the Spirit, he leads us directly into how we should approach our brother who may be "caught in any transgression." He doesn't suggest we pinch his head off. Instead, he instructs us how to lovingly and kindly help *restore* him. In correction, we want a result of restoration, not a feeling of guilt. Paul carefully chose his wording. Restoration denotes a healing change, where guilt weighs heavy and scars instead of healing. We are a people who jump into correction, and often we allow our opinions to lead our methods. A child sometimes needs a harsher discipline, but adults are certainly less receptive to finger wagging. Rather than listening, they grow defensive, and their hearts close to any guidance.

Paul tells us that those with spiritual maturity and a spirit of gentleness should take the lead. He encourages us not to condemn but be gentle and humble. He doesn't imply we lessen the severity of the transgression but that we approach the subject to restore. Teach from the consequence of the sin. Those in the wrong cannot deny the result. This was how Jesus taught, with stories and examples of the result of the action. These led people to make logical and restorative changes to their behaviors. Lastly, Paul leaves us with a warning. Watch out for ourselves that we do not fall into sin too. Guide with restoration in mind. Watch your own behavior. The result of the work is long-lasting.

Finally, brothers, whatever is true, whatever is honorable,
whatever is just, whatever is pure, whatever is lovely,
whatever is commendable, if there is any excellence,
if there is anything worthy of praise, think about these things.
—Philippians 4:8

People are going to disagree and struggle with making the right decision. It's just life. Yet, how we respond in these times sets a standard. Whether it is the workplace or the church, our response to conflict is essential.

Everyone who knows we live by godly standards observes our responses and actions. They are quick to judge us when we meet with weaknesses. Paul tells us to let our reasonableness show. As the peace of God covers us by His love, we must make the effort to keep a good name and relationship with others. Paul knew people were always watching. Yet, in the worst of his situations, he rejoiced. Others always saw the unexpected parts of his love of Christ. Self-control. Joy. Peace in every situation.

We will not always agree, but we can always control our responses and how we make decisions. Before you take aim at someone, consider your reply using Philippians 4:8 as a guide. Ask if this action is honorable, true, just, pure, lovely, and commendable. If the answer is yes, your decision or behavior is right. It is not always easy, but it allows the opportunity that others will see a person who reflects a Christlike attitude.

Christ wants us to resolve conflicts. Resolution sometimes means meeting in the middle or simply agreeing to disagree. The point is how do others perceive the life of a Christian? We are not to be weak or wishy-washy but Christlike. Jesus was never weak in His beliefs or stances, but He showed great strength through His love. What do others see in you?

Day 82

Even as the Son of Man came not to be served but to serve,
and to give his life as a ransom for many.
—Matthew 20:28

I sn't it just like a good momma to want to know the rewards of her children? They work hard to train their children, to see them grow and develop into fine adults. Of course, any good mother wants to see her children recognized. Such as it was with the wife of Zebedee, the mother of James and John. Jesus lovingly called them the Sons of Thunder.

Competitive in all they did, it was no surprise they would want to know who would sit on either side of Jesus in heaven, but Jesus quickly thwarted that. He asked, "Are you able to drink the cup that I am to drink?" Boldly they said yes. Even at that proclamation, it didn't seem they understood the cup to which Jesus referred. His death—His suffering that was to come.

Jesus's followers still believed that His kingdom was worldly. He had to address this issue and clarify that His kingdom was heavenly. He had come to serve. There was no throne, no position of authority in man's earthly kingdom, but Jesus would serve and serve without lording over others. Service would be a reflection of Jesus. Jesus's mindset differed from the years these men waited for the Messiah, the Messiah they thought would be an earthly king like Solomon. They would have to learn, and in time, they came to understand the cup from which Jesus drank. Even today, man has difficulty looking past their earthly desires to grasp what it means to be a servant: to care for the souls of others and bring them into belief. This is what Christ did. In this process of example, He taught what a servant looked like. From healing to cooking breakfast on the shore, Jesus served with His whole heart. Servanthood is an attitude of the heart and a work of the hands. Release your idea of what a servant is and get down into the business of Christ. Be a reflection of Jesus.

Day 83

From of old no one has heard or perceived by the ear,
no eye has seen a God besides you, who acts for
those who wait for him.
—Isaiah 64:4

I saiah addressed the nation of Israel at a time when they had fallen away. They'd begun to worship idols, false gods, and participate in pagan rituals. It was clear who God was to the believers. Still, His wonders were hidden from those who had pushed God to the side. Who and what God was didn't suit their sinful desires, so they turned away and lost sight of His blessings then and to come. For the remainder of believers, Isaiah encouraged them to stand firm and hold on. He reminded them of the Messiah to come and the multitude of blessings stored up for them. They couldn't begin to imagine, no ear had heard, no eye had seen, what God had in store for those who patiently wait. It was hard to see that God continued to work on their behalves. He never stops working for His people. He may not give us all the details, but His work for our welfare continues, and the results happen in our waiting.

Waiting isn't one of man's better attributes. When we pray, we expect the answer now. When the answers are slow, we take on the task of making things work out in our interests, or we assume God has brushed off our needs. In our greed to have things work to our benefits, we may become blind to God's work on our behalves. Isaiah, and later Paul (in 1 Corinthians 2:9), reiterated the importance of waiting. They encouraged the people to wait because there is so much more than they can ever know. The wonders of God are hidden from those who do not believe. Our belief and our waiting on Him open that door for us. God is working for you. Be patient. Your ears have not heard nor your eyes have not seen who acts for those who wait on Him.

Day 84

Truly, truly, I say to you, a servant is not greater than his master,
nor is a messenger greater than the one who sent him.
If you know these things, blessed are you if you do them.
—John 13:16–17

With his small son next to him, a man shoved his wife and shouted, "You're nothing. You're worthless." Later, the mother corrected her son for taking a toy from his brother at home. Her small son shoved her and shouted, "You're nothing. You're worthless." Children learn from example. What they see, they emulate.

Jesus knew His time was ending. It was the feast of the Passover. His disciples gathered to share a meal. This would be a final opportunity for Jesus to teach the children by example. The custom was for a servant to wash the feet of the guests. Perhaps through divine preparation, there was no servant present to do this. Jesus, instead, wrapped a towel around His waist, picked up a basin of water, and then commenced washing the disciples' feet—even against the protest of Peter. His heart was in the right place. He respected Jesus and could not see Him doing the work of a servant. Jesus must have smiled at Peter's naivete, understanding he meant well. But there was a more significant meaning. There were immense lessons involved. Not only was Jesus teaching the disciples what it means to be a servant, but it was a foretelling of their ministries to the people. They would not be crowned with great titles or prestigious positions, theirs would be a position of servanthood, being as much like Jesus as they could.

Jesus sent a strong message to His disciples as He stooped to His knees to wash the dirt from their feet. He identified Himself as the Master, but He proved He was not greater than His Father. In this simple act, Jesus taught humility, love, and servanthood. We are no greater than the Master. Emulate His example and serve your brothers and sisters.

Week 13—His Work in Me

The challenges that lie before you are not easy tasks. We've noted before, God never promised that a life with Him would be easy. It is, however, rewarding, both here and in eternity.

When Jesus gave His great commission, it wasn't just to the disciples. He gave that commission for all those who followed, all believers regardless of age, sex, or race. God divinely created the entirety of the universe to be His, to rejoice in Him, and to glorify Him. There was not one detail in His order left undone. Every part of this universe works in accordance with who He is.

Do you recognize the depth of His love? Has it truly occurred to you what He offers you? This God of love, salvation, and eternity longs for a relationship with you. Open your eyes. Stop being blinded by the things the world tries to push on to you. Be His. Abide in Him, and He will abide in you.

As we conclude these ninety days of study, challenge yourself to want to know Him deeper. Make it a point to not miss out on being what He draws you to be. Reestablish a strong Christian worldview by first beginning with prayer and then by doing what you have been taught to do, get into the Word. Put on your spiritual armor and make a stand.

Day 85

For we do not wrestle against flesh and blood, but
against . . . rulers, . . . authorities, . . . cosmic powers, . . .
spiritual forces of evil in the heavenly places. Therefore
take up the whole armor of God, that you may be
able to withstand in the evil day.
—Ephesians 6:12–13

Many are quick to attach the title of "spiritual warfare" to any difficulty they might experience. Rather than being an actual spiritual attack, it can be an *easy out* for the hardships of life, even an excuse for the consequence of bad decisions. Before you press the title of spiritual warfare onto a problematic situation, be sure it truly is.

This is not to lessen the severity of a spiritual attack. Instead, it's to be sure we recognize the immensity of it. Paul's description of the tools available to us for our spiritual protection is one of his best. He brings a great understanding of the power available to us through the gifts of God—the Word, the truth, righteousness, readiness, faith, salvation, and he helps make them applicable to us by calling them armor. What better way for us to grasp hold of these tools, these gifts, and what better way to learn how to use them.

It is no secret that the cosmic battle over evil reels above us in a realm we cannot see, but it's essential to understand these battles are not in heaven. They are in the spiritual realm. Here the battle led by Christ takes place, and His defenses are wielded here. But our defense should not rely solely on the cosmic battle. We must do our part with the specific tools that protect and arm us for the spiritual attack that will come. Satan does his best to thwart any attempt to move God's kingdom forward. In those times, he will rain down attacks to frustrate, detour, or end our work. Take up your armor and fight the battle. You have the tools. Now go on the defense.

Day 86

Whoever pursues righteousness and kindness will find life,
righteousness, and honor.
—Proverbs 21:21

"Righteousness and kindness" (some texts refer to kindness as mercy). Do you understand these? It's vital to ask and know what righteousness and kindness or mercy are. Simply put, righteousness is behaving and being in agreement with God's standards of right and wrong. Mercy is the compassion and forgiveness given to those who may not rightfully deserve it. Once we know these simplistic definitions, we can address the Proverbs scripture.

Imagine being Solomon and having God offer him anything and then choosing wisdom. What a difficult choice. Did he realize what accompanies wisdom, yet he chose that anyway? Either way, this line in Proverbs is very profound. Remember the meanings and then reread the text. Both righteousness and kindness (mercy) are two challenging things. Living according to God's idea of right and wrong sometimes clashes with our human thought—processes. We tend to justify the things in our lives that we innately know are wrong by God's standard. The world tries to confuse us on gender and sexuality by forcing us to concede to their justification, when in fact God is clear on every count.

Furthermore, why be merciful or truly kind to those who have wronged us? They hurt us. There is no room for forgiveness. But God's standard is to do so.

These are the things the world wants you to believe, and when we do, we lose sight of God's ideas of righteousness and kindness. God's ways are simple, but at the same time, they are the most difficult because they buck the general thoughts of humanity. Hurt means repaying hurt. Justify what is wrong and do it in God's name. Christian, tread carefully. Seek righteousness and kindness as God means it. Practice both, and the blessing of righteousness and honor follow.

"And you shall love the Lord your God with all your heart and with all your soul and with all your mind and with all your strength." The second is this: "You shall love your neighbor as yourself." There is no other commandment greater than these.
—Mark 12:30–31

Do you love yourself, or are you your own worst enemy? It's an important question to ponder, but we need to read the complete text to know this scripture fully and see it from a deeper perspective. Love your God is the priority, and then love your neighbor as yourself is second.

Jesus made no bones about answering the scribe's question as to which of these commandments were the most important. Jesus noted just prior that God was "one." That fact knocked down the walls of doubt about Himself that the scribe might have felt. But there is a deeper perspective.

It's easy to get these things out of order. Our human tendency is to place ourselves above others, even above God, but this is not what Jesus is stressing. Put the priorities in order. Love God, and then love your neighbor as you love yourself. Many will cringe at that, but it's something to consider seriously. It goes back to the heart of the servant. Jesus served. He loved others above Himself, and as a result, lives were changed.

Do you love yourself appropriately, and in that love, can you see how you can love others even more? Too much love for yourself makes for selfishness. Not enough makes for a deterioration of the heart. When the pendulum swings too far in either direction, we do not love the way we should.

Our love for God is first, and when that compass points correctly, the love for those around us balances. When you feel your compass needle leaning, redirect. Love God first. Truly love yourself appropriately, and then love your neighbor as you love yourself.

He who descended is the one who also ascended far above all the
heavens, that he might fill all things. And he gave the apostles, the
prophets, the evangelists, the shepherds and teachers, to equip the saints
for the work of ministry, for building up the body of Christ.
—Ephesians 4:10–14

As Christians, we tend to look at what Christ did during His descension, when He left heaven and came to earth as flesh: "And the Word became flesh and dwelt among us" (John 1:14). We look at His earthly ministry, death, and resurrection, but this scripture's real meat comes in the word *ascended*. Christ's ascension completed the promise of the Messiah. The prophecy was fulfilled. But before Jesus left earth to take His seat at the right hand of God, He gave gifts. Some were apostles, some prophets, evangelists, shepherds to the flock, and teachers. That is not where the gifts ended. Before you were born, God knew who you were. He knew your strengths, weaknesses, tenacities, and faithfulness. Before He released you into your mother's womb, God gifted you with what He knew He could use in and through you.

We tend to only look at those who have talents like singing, playing an instrument, or even writing as being gifted. That is just how shortsighted we are, for God gifted us all with something unique. Though this scripture refers to the gifts given to prepare those for service and ministry, it's safe to say whatever your gift is can be used as a ministry. Some are gifted listeners, advisors, helpers, you name it. Generally, your gift is found in your passion God uses that gift when you open your heart. Indeed, God doesn't send His servants out for His work unprepared. He prepares you. Open your heart to His calling. He has already gifted you.

Day 89

And I heard every creature in heaven and on earth and under the earth
and in the sea, and all that is in them, saying,
"To him who sits on the throne and to the Lamb be blessing and honor
and glory and might forever and ever!"
—Revelation 5:13

Imagine John in his amazement as he viewed a glimpse of the last day. Try to wrap your mind around things so great, so immense, so magnificent—even frightening, and then sit down to describe them as best you can. Imagine how he must have felt. Honored. Joyful. Afraid.

During the 2020 presidential debate between former vice-president Joe Biden and Vermont's senator Bernie Sanders, a commercial aired on CNN. Ron Reagan Jr., son of former president Ronald Reagan Sr., proudly professed he was a devout atheist and proclaimed he was "not afraid to burn in hell." It was hard to take in. How could anyone not be afraid to burn in hell? This was the ultimate opportunity for Satan to kick the Christian worldview to the curb. Why should anyone be frightened if Ron Reagan Jr. isn't afraid of hell? It was a sad moment, and God's heart must have ached. After all, He doesn't want to lose even one. Not one!

As Christians, we know how this story ends, and though we didn't have the view John experienced, we certainly have the Word that gives us a decent picture. There will be no doubters when Christ comes. No one who can stand and say God is fake. When the gates of hell open and the flames shoot into the air, those brash enough to say they are not afraid to burn in hell will hear, "Depart from me."

Creation knows the King of Kings. The mountains, the oceans, the sky. Every animal. Every creature that crawls knows God Almighty. There is no denying the Creator, the Ruler, the God of the universe, for He will reign forever and ever. We have an eternity in heaven to look forward to, so we take a just knee and lift our hearts in praise. Glory to God in the highest.

Day 90

If my people who are called by my name humble themselves, and pray
and seek my face and turn from their wicked ways, then I will hear from
heaven and will forgive their sin and heal their land.
—2 Chronicles 7:14

I t was the dedication of the temple Solomon built. He stood before the people, before God, and offered a prayer for blessing over this place of worship and God's people. And God responded: He said to humble themselves and pray, and He would hear and forgive their sin. He would heal their land. Imagine what Solomon must have thought. Would the people, off and on in their faithfulness, obey to receive the blessings?

Finding God begins with humility. Willingly admitting we are sinful is tough, and it dents our pride. Prayer follows, but it's the kind of prayer that is more than skin deep. It's relationally deep. It's honest, grateful, even heart-wrenching. Our prayer opens the floodgates of heaven for all that God has stored. Though today's churches offer fantastic music, good messages, and even fancy lights and productions, those are not the things He asks. God asks for our humility, prayer, and repentance. He asks for our hearts and that we glorify Him. That means laying out our sin and seeking His forgiveness, followed by a change.

God knew then, and He still knows His people will sin, and here He reminded His people and us that there is *always* a way back to Him. A way in which He loves and responds, but it means going to our knees. Our Father has always offered His love freely, but we are frail and weak, easily tempted and swayed. However, if we humble ourselves, pray, seek His face, and turn from sin, He will hear and heal. He will forgive. As you pray, think about the lifeline it provides. Seek Him. Love Him. He is always nearby.

Final Thoughts to Ponder

As you have studied these devotions, note that they are not written from a first person or *I* perspective. This is intentional, and here is why. Our Christian worldview is slipping in the world and within our body of believers. It hasn't happened overnight, but it began hundreds of years ago, a constant nipping away at the absolutes of God. We can thank a progressive world for making this more apparent now that we have social media, worldwide communication, and constant news programming. What was once a silent monger is now vibrant and evident simply because we have 24/7 access to current information.

This is good and bad because now it's no longer silent. Instead, this slow gnawing away has become a screaming evil attacking us from every angle. In the devotions you've read and studied, I did not want them to be about me or my experiences. I wanted them to strictly put us back into the Word and put us there uninhibited.

I doubt you will have found a sweetness in the voice in which these are written, instead, an intensity of looking just below the surface. My prayer was not that we would fall into a doctrinal debate or go so deep into the apologetics that we would lose interest, but that we would take a layman's look at the layer right below the surface. We need the milk and the meat of the Scripture in a way we could apply it. For that reason, you have not seen the first-person pronoun of *I*. It's not about me. It is about us reconnecting, suckling on the milk, chewing on the meat, and developing a hunger for our Abba Father again. It is about perspective. Seeking, taking the Scripture we frequently see to examine it, and establishing a habit of daily study and communication with God.

We've all been affected by the desensitization of the world. Little by little, the standards we once held to are compromised. Convenience has become an enemy of work and a friend of entitlement. A lack of modesty, our love of entertainment and sports, our desire for wealth, and loss of benevolence are all fueled by our wants and desires—what makes us happy over what is godly.

Simply put, I wanted us back into the Word by choice. By desire. By a hunger. I wanted a devotional that you could pick up at any season of life, man or woman, and find that it perfectly suits your current situation. We all know that every answer under the sun is in the Word. We cannot begin to reestablish a solid Christian worldview outside the church's walls until we have established a firm worldview and foundation inside our hearts. I desired to reintroduce you to the Word. The first step to reconnecting spiritually with God. If we can do that, if we have begun that in this work, then hopefully, a flame reignites and the blaze will rise in your spirit. Hopefully, you will realize the joy of being on fire for Christ. Then and only then can we begin to reestablish a solid Christian worldview outside the walls of the church building.

As we close this work, I hope you will agree that the basis of anything we begin is found in the power of prayer.

Notes

1. Linda Lyons, "No Heroes in the Beltway," Gallup.com, July 30, 2002, https://news.gallup.com/poll/6487/heroes-beltway.aspx.
2. Brian Arnold, "If Christ Is Risen, Nothing Else Matters," Phoenix Seminary, April 12, 2020, https://ps.edu/if-christ-is-risen-nothing-else-matters/.
3. *The Truth Project*, "Lesson Two: Philosophy & Ethics: Says Who?" (2006, Focus on the Family) DVD series.
4. D. W. Whittle, "I Know Not Why God's Wondrous Grace," 1883, https://hymnary.org/text/i_know_not_why_gods_wondrous_grace_to_me.

If you enjoyed this book, will you consider sharing the message with others?

Let us know your thoughts. You can let the author know by visiting or sharing a photo of the cover on our social media pages or leaving a review at a retailer's site. All of it helps us get the message out!

Email: info@ironstreammedia.com

 @ironstreammedia

---

Iron Stream, Iron Stream Fiction, Iron Stream Kids, Brookstone Publishing Group, and Life Bible Study are imprints of Iron Stream Media, which derives its name from Proverbs 27:17, "As iron sharpens iron, so one person sharpens another." This sharpening describes the process of discipleship, one to another. With this in mind, Iron Stream Media provides a variety of solutions for churches, ministry leaders, and nonprofits ranging from in-depth Bible study curriculum and Christian book publishing to custom publishing and consultative services.

For more information on ISM and its imprints, please visit IronStreamMedia.com